The Moneypower Continuum

The Moneypower Continuum

An Extended Essay on Money and Power in Religion, Education, Politics, and Business

FRANCIS X. HEALY JR.

iUniverse LLC
Bloomington

The Moneypower Continuum
An Extended Essay on Money and Power in Religion, Education, Politics, and Business

Copyright © 2012 by Francis X. Healy Jr.

All rights reserved. No part of this book may be used or reproduced by any means, graphic, electronic, or mechanical, including photocopying, recording, taping or by any information storage retrieval system without the written permission of the publisher except in the case of brief quotations embodied in critical articles and reviews.

iUniverse books may be ordered through booksellers or by contacting:

iUniverse LLC
1663 Liberty Drive
Bloomington, IN 47403
www.iuniverse.com
1-800-Authors (1-800-288-4677)

Because of the dynamic nature of the Internet, any web addresses or links contained in this book may have changed since publication and may no longer be valid. The views expressed in this work are solely those of the author and do not necessarily reflect the views of the publisher, and the publisher hereby disclaims any responsibility for them.

Any people depicted in stock imagery provided by Thinkstock are models, and such images are being used for illustrative purposes only.
Certain stock imagery © Thinkstock.

ISBN: 978-1-4759-3119-8 (sc)
ISBN: 978-1-4759-3121-1 (hc)
ISBN: 978-1-4759-3120-4 (ebk)

Printed in the United States of America

iUniverse rev. date: 06/04/2012

For the Antichrist is the worst beast. He destroys people who deny him.
He joins himself to kings, dukes, and wealthy ones.

Hildegard of Bingen, Scivias: Third Part, Vision 11:27

This book is dedicated to my life, in order of its appearance:

Dolores

    Frank

    Mark

    Jennifer

               Julia Rose

                Christopher Francis

Introduction

I suspect this book may have arisen from an unconscious need buried in my psyche. I completed the course work for a PhD in economics many years ago. Then I decided to do it again in political science. In neither case did I write a dissertation. There were various reasons why not, but ultimately it was a good thing. I avoided some problems by not having the degree later in life, and I gained some advantages. I do have good excuses for not writing the dissertation. While I was taking the courses, I was working full time at increasingly responsible positions. I was also teaching courses in the evening at either the University of Pennsylvania or at LaSalle University in Philadelphia. Perhaps, I thought finally, I had learned enough, did not need the degrees, and went on with the balance of my lifetime of education on my own.

So this book might serve partially and unconsciously as my dissertation in either discipline, without the severe academic trappings. It is not what I had in mind as I wrote it.

When I was eighteen years old, just old enough to join the Knights of Columbus, I did. I have belonged to very few voluntary organizations of any kind in my life, and when I did, it was usually for reasons less than in accord with the noble aims of the group.

The Knights of Columbus offered opportunities for beer consumption at low prices. A barrel was tapped. A dollar was thrown into a glass on the bar, and beer was available until the barrel was emptied.

I joined a fraternity in college not so much for brotherhood but because its parties were an inexpensive date. I had little money, and this was a fraternity without resources such as a house, so dues were very low.

I was not an indifferent member of either my fraternity or the Knights. I was vice president of the fraternity. I attended meetings and other functions of the Knights. I even marched in the Saint Patrick's Day parade with them. Only a few years later, I could not have imagined doing such a thing.

I was incredulous about the intensity of engagement of the older men in the Knights. Offices were coveted and sharply contested. Committee chairmanships were likewise regarded as badges of high honor. Ceremonials were meticulously conducted. As a kid, I just didn't get it. There are larger things in life.

I later realized that most of the men did not have interesting lives. We were largely working-class people. The older men enjoyed not much of economic luxuries or workplace authority, and so the organization assumed importance in their lives. I saw this as a good thing. I really liked these men, but I should not see their circumstances in the same light of my youth when looking back at them today. If I had a condescending attitude, it had little foundation. It was undoubtedly based on my personal expectations, not on my circumstances of the time.

Now that I am more than four times the age of my eligibility for the K of C, I live in a community whose residents are required to be fifty-five years or older. We have an elected board of our Homeowners' Association, and various committees charged with functions such as landscaping, recreation, finance, and other matters.

There is a difference now. This is a community of expensive homes. Most residents have had successful careers, and many are still working at them. Businessmen, consultants, lawyers, engineers, medical doctors, teachers, researchers, civil servants, and similar occupations are well represented here.

It does take me back to the Knights of Columbus. Board memberships are sharply contested in elections, committee memberships and chairs are coveted, enemies are created, rivalries sting, and the gamut of politics, formal and informal, is run. Not much mellowing with age.

Over a period of time, the noted sharply contested board seats have become less coveted. It could return at any time. Beyond that, the remaining notes on politics still hold. I suspect that the underlying, sometimes very nasty, politics are why many residents are not interested in becoming elected to the board.

A plausible reason for all this might be that retired people need these activities. It doesn't hold. A substantial number of active participants in the game are employed. I don't get it. Even in insignificant places, power has a way of influencing its wielders, I suppose.

This work has two themes—power and mythology. The preceding anecdotes show that the tiny Knights of Columbus and a homeowners' association share these motifs with the huge institutions of my concern.

1

The Bigger Ones

As humanity moves toward whatever our destination is to be, we have constructed essential institutions to aid us with the journey. The oversized ones—church, state, and corporation—are a strong influence on us that we sometimes realize and at other times do not. There are other secondary institutions of considerable importance as well. Education in its formal garb is a notable one. It weaves through all the others. I call education secondary only in the sense that we do a remarkable job of ignoring it personally. When we finish our inadequate formal schooling, we can safely disregard any further educational efforts. And most of us do. We cannot ignore the other three. Like it or not, church affects us whether we are believers or atheists.

We have many ways of thinking about, or understanding, our institutions. Much of what we "know" is belief rather than knowledge. Mythology is a great part of what we think about everything, including ourselves. The standard myths about the named institutions are often far off the mark. Here I am going to examine some of the realities of these institutions, recognizing that I may only be attempting to establish another set of myths. I hope not.

What must be understood about any institution, from the sacred to the profane, is that they most often serve the purposes of those in control. The people who are in control are not necessarily those who are formally designated as being in charge. Adding to the mystery of institutions, stated purposes and philosophies are secondary. These are masks to legitimize the institution that rapidly get atrophied as mythology. A common example that has come, once again, dramatically to the fore is the separation of ownership and control in the corporation. The legal owners are the stockholders, but rarely do they have any control over the affairs of the corporation. As early as 1932 Berle and Means, in *The Modern Corporation and Private Property*, provided us with the landmark study on this subject—the impotence of stockholders in affecting decisions made by corporate managers. I say as early as 1932, because the corporation of that time was neither as powerful nor as extensive an institution as it has become today. The earliest ones to resemble today's corporations were founded only in the 1890s. The railroads in the United States were the first (Kessner, 96). The railroads molded the early history of corporate America. Indeed, the railroads *were* the early history of corporate America. Throughout that early corporate history, these railroads were virtually the only large corporations run as private businesses. That is interesting for several reasons. They were powerful monopolies. They depended on power grants from government. This a pattern that is so common in corporate history that the role of free markets run as businesses in freewheeling competition on their own is a basic myth in our economy.

Yet not much has changed as applied to the character of problems of control in the corporation since Berle and Means. The problem has gotten worse as corporate powers have expanded and intensified. Other organizations are similarly split between ownership and control, or the ostensible aims and beneficiaries and the actual. There is an easy explanation of why the divergence is always present. It is the moneypower continuum.

The moneypower continuum is the complete identification of money and power. Even where the mythology suggests otherwise, such as in religious institutions, this identity is pervasive. Acquiring one is the same as acquiring the other. This was not always so with mankind. In early societies where there was no money, much less wealth, power was something apart. With time, the association became common. The earlier societies did have the continuum, but it was vested in a very small group and usually was a local or regional occurrence. Even in more recent times, apparently honest political leaders were not given to accumulations of huge sums of money, or they had no access to them. Winston Churchill's widow had to survive on a very small pension. We can look at many political leaders, great and not so great, who never became wealthy. The difference today is attributable to the existence, incredible growth and influence of that huge money machine, the corporation. Its relationship to, and additional accumulation of, political power has changed everything. It has created the moneypower continuum. It is my thesis that it effectually has taken over politics. It may soon be the successor form to national governments, in fact. It is strides beyond national governments. It has a global spread. It does not, of course, thereby offer anything of the goals of traditional world government advocates.

Huge numbers of people do not share in the apparent benefits of the continuum. At the same time, the numbers who do are larger than ever. Those who are aware of it in some way also have grown, as have those who aspire to and lust for its benefits.

As the various institutions to be examined were created and grew, the continuum was also created and was integral to them. It was embellished and strengthened with growth. Regarding the present and recent history, the influence and pervasiveness of communications is the theme running through much of the difficulties that I address. This will be noted more than once. It is a critical distinguishing influence. It is without precedence. While money and power, and their close association, are not altogether a recent phenomenon, their fantastic enlargement is.

Another aspect of the continuum is its threading through the institutions themselves. I roughly consider their relationships as beginning with church, with academy following close on, then state, and, finally, corporation. They each operate in the moneypower continuum. Consequently, church, state, and academy become more like corporations and corporations take on the methods of these three as suits their purposes. In all cases, much is traceable to the basic moneypower continuum.

The academy, mainly in higher education, has become naked business. The lofty goals of education once known and believed are submerged deeply into profit and loss statements, usually couched in other language, but not always. I looked at the website of a university and saw something called an Integrated Marketing Task Force. Its mission was to develop "a unifying theme that will serve as a reference point for our mission and values." That says a lot about what education is all about. Points for naked honesty should be awarded here, but I naively still think that university missions and values should be defined by something other than marketing. There should be at least a pretense to loftier foundations for values. Have they no shame? Of course not.

Today you don't see many powerful politicians who are poor. Neither are powerful religious leaders or university presidents. There are few wealthy heads of corporations who disdain power. Their power lust is not simply that which would be exercised within the corporation. It is much like government power in character. It often goes to other places as well. The corporation is the apex of the evolution of the continuum. It is also the tentacled course of the continuum through the other institutions, such as universities, churches, operas, orchestras, and so on.

The associated money and power of the continuum are the combined quest and objective of practically all institutions. The few where it is not found are rarities, and they become rarer as time and our worldviews become more entrenched in the continuum. Many groups and organizations that formerly carried at least a facade of being above the muck and mire of power and money are clearly open about it today. I have noted the nature of the university. Many professions, such as the medical and legal, are examples. Professional sports are pure business monopolies. Sports are a good example of newly created institutions moving into the continuum. They are immensely involved with money and power. They are fed with talent from the universities and have been instrumental in creating universities as businesses. At the college level of "sportsmanship," their educational values are dishonesty and violence. The goal of athletics exclusively is to win. The intensity of the objective leads to moral compromise, and many students who participate in athletics use any means they can get away with. Sometimes this results in public scandal. The day-to-day minor cheating and rough play do not attract much attention. In fact, these are all considered part of the game. These values carry forward into the places where the "amateur" athletes and their old and young fans find themselves in pursuit of moneypower. It is the core of professional athletics. Professional sports derive most of their huge incomes from television and government subsidies as well as special legal exemptions granted by government. They are the perfect model of a new thing incorporating the worst of the new things. Sports have been around for centuries. Their intense involvement in money and power is relatively recent. Consider only the international Olympic Games as an example. Others abound.

Note that I use money as the meld with power. Not wealth, economics, or the more rational bases that money measures. The grasp is for money. It reaches obscene levels of pursuit having little to do directly with wealth or ordinary economic objectives. Whether we speak of university endowments or patent ownerships; insane salaries of corporate executives (a fantastic kind of super misers), the regal and financial trappings of churchmen, the temporarily devoted public servants who then recycle their devotion to the corporations they aided in their devoted public service, it is integral to pure power pursuit. There is no difference between the drive for power or control and the drive for money. Numerous examples illustrate this point, and all institutions, however noble or ignoble their goals, show how it works. They may be distinguished by whether they approach the continuum from the money or the power perspective. This is not a really important distinction. The myth coloration is different depending on which end is at the front. Politicians are supposed to seek power for our good. Business executives are supposed to seek money. Realistically, there is no difference between them. Their aims come to the same target. It is, as I posit, a continuum. Results of the game are the same. Those in control enhance their monetary and power assets in some way as the first order of church, academy, government, or corporation. There are always wonderful reasons why they do this, from saving our souls to causing the marvels of economic growth for our good. As they progress, the high ideals become more flimsy. Few of us are really fooled. But we accept.

Some general examples will be explained and then expanded, but first I will offer some detail on the moneypower continuum. The power ingredient is shown in the many ways that money loses its functions as viewed by its pursuers. Textbook descriptions of the functions for money are that it is a medium of exchange, a means of stored value, and a standard of value. (Bush's Secretary of the Treasury John W. Snow, when questioned about his views on how the dollar should be managed when its value was declining in international markets, responded with this textbook list. I thought he was evading the question by sarcasm, but the press did not treat his answer that way. Where do we find these men?) Considering the huge sums of money about which this book is concerned, there is no way it can be seriously regarded as bearing a relationship to economic goods and services. That is secondary. The use of money for purchasing necessities or even luxuries in the extreme are far surpassed by the accumulations by those manipulating the continuum from whatever base. It fades into its own existence, totally unrelated to economics. Ultimately, it creates a series of economies, to be described later, and thereby demolishes anything that can be understood as "the economy." This creates many large, ugly problems for humanity.

A good example of money losing its functions as we usually see them is the regular casino gambler, especially addicts. They see money as something quite apart from its usual functions. It is exclusively a token of power. Little wonder that governments, the usual site of power, eagerly establish various gambling establishments to rob the poor. Thus it is with many others throughout the "respectable" world.

Other brief examples make the point:

- Religious organizations are continually engaged in political activities internally and externally, accompanied by the accumulation of financial resources as very much a part of the package.
- Universities are run blatantly as businesses, with their administrations dedicated to expanding their markets and acquiring power just as a business corporation does.
- Politics, which is supposed to be the study and practice of bargaining and power, is impossible to consider without its immersion in huge sums of money.

Corporations have ascended into power and money—accumulation never seen before.

Certainly, religious organizations, universities, and political institutions must be economically viable. The point here is that they go well beyond basics, and are pursuing money profits, though usually they call them something else. Moreover, in this pursuit, they become more like corporations in form, methods, and goals, taking on the shortcomings of corporations and debasing their own characters. It's not a matter of appropriate criticism to imply that any institution other than business institutions should ignore economic realities. That would be foolish. The problem has become that they are in pursuit of economic goals to the detriment of their real purposes, and this results in tremendous deterioration of values. They all become rivals.

Is there anything new about all this? Not on its face. Here is a quote from Thomas Kessner's *Capital City* (183):

He had assembled a portfolio that included the telegraph monopoly, the coveted central link of the transcontinental railroad, New York's rapid transit monopoly, and a number of important Western railroads, as well as a newspaper. In his hands he held a substantial part of America's new economy. There was no end to (Jay) Gould's greed and power plays.

The time was 1881. Imagine. They had a "new economy" way back then. And we all thought that the new economy did not arrive until slightly more than one hundred years thereafter and that it has already expired. The late nineteenth century was a time when the corporation had just begun to assume the form into which it has evolved, or, if you prefer, been intelligently designed.

Is there anything wrong about it? There is much wrong about it. Probably not much is new about it, but it is such a different world today that the effects now are worth reconsidering. Granted that every age sees itself as different from others, with little firm evidence to support that view, but there are some dramatic differences about life as we live it today. It is almost cliché to note the world's differences over relatively few years of recent history, but it is in fact a sharply different place. Television and the Internet show us an entirely new world. Everybody knows everything, which really means everybody knows nothing. Surfeits of information available are not really digested by their recipients. News has become just another form of entertainment. It is the world village of gossip, but there are no other village characteristics, such as neighborliness, that go along with it. Missing in this array is widespread serious thought—an outcome of our strange world as well as reinforcing its character.

The immense scale and reach of major organizations is deeper and wider than ever before. This in itself adds an environment to humanity that is entirely new also. I cover our instruments of the moneypower continuum in the rough sequence of their emergence in human affairs. In some respects they were all simultaneously in existence for most of human history. Their separate existence, or creation, traces their place in the continuum and the simultaneous enlargement of their moneypower. The exception is the academy, which has never had great moneypower standing compared with the other three. Still, the academy follows in the mold and is not without either the trappings of moneypower or the influence that it accords in society.

My emphasis is mainly on the institutions of the United States. But clearly much of the treatment and conclusions apply widely over the world. The relative place of the four institutions will vary elsewhere. Thus, church is comparable in stature and control in some places today as it was in Europe of centuries past, but not in Europe today.

The reason for the geography of concern is similar to the answer Willie Sutton gave regarding why he robbed banks. He is said to have replied, that's where the money (and in our case, the money and the power) is.

2

Church

Consider an institution in which many subunits have been plagued by terrible scandals that have come to light with wide press coverage. Numerous accusations are heard, and it is learned that this organization has covered up these problems for many years by paying off victims. It has not infrequently allowed the perpetrators to continue in similar positions where they may continue their scandalous and harmful activities.

Various successful lawsuits have been brought against this organization, costing multimillions in compensation to victims. The organization has threatened to seek bankruptcy or in fact has declared bankruptcy in some instances, for protection. It has mostly said little for public information in the midst of this storm.

One of its most egregious and well-known leaders flees the country to another, where he is certain he will not be extradited should he be indicted. Several of the lesser operatives do the same, and in their cases when a state attorney general sends an inquiry to the secretary of state of the sheltering country, it is returned unopened.

Rogue head of a major corporation? WorldCom? Enron? No, it is the Catholic Church in America. The Vatican is its refuge.

The horrendous scandals in the United States have led to utterly unrelated debates, to the extent that there are debates within the church on subjects such as celibacy. Pedophilia is undoubtedly no respecter of marriage vows, so this is just so much nonsense.

What is somewhat amusing is the notoriety of our highly Catholic neighbor to the south and the women of whom their priests are so fond. Perhaps formal release from celibacy would help there. But there are no signs that the Vatican wishes to look into the problem there, any more than it did regarding the problem of the United States until it became impossible to pretend it wasn't there.

The circumstances of the Catholic Church in the United States are a blatant illustration of the moneypower continuum in religion in our time. It is hardly the only one.

Christianity began its involvement with the continuum right at the outset, and with well-remembered notoriety. Those pieces of silver that were exchanged for fingering its founder, who was seen as a threat to the powers in control, are known by everyone. The episode also illustrates the futility of the pursuit of greed, which is the heart of the continuum. In this case, both parties to the exchange eventually lost. The religion flourished, and the fingerer died a nasty death.

The earliest and most powerful control over mankind has been religion. It has often been the sum of other institutions that we will examine. The church has been the state. It has been the heart of business practices and the strict rule setter for other business enterprises. It has been the only formal education institution. Indeed, the divorce of secular higher education, at least in the Western world, from religion is something of relatively recent history. There are still colleges designated as related to various faiths, but most of them are indistinguishable from secular colleges in practice. If they put much emphasis on their religious origins, marketing suffers. This does not include those schools steeped in the learning of the religious wrong. (The group we usually call the religious right.)

Throughout most of human history, all of the things that happened in society were either directly managed or powerfully influenced by religion. The church has been the continuum in all its aspects. It has been the state, the academy, and the corporation (i.e., business originally). The academy and the corporation have spun off. The opportunities were too great, and the new forms of the continuum enlarged that continuum substantially. Church has degenerated into a special interest group, even if a sometimes powerful one. The academy exists by the sufferance of the corporation. Eventually, the state will become a special interest group to the corporation rather than the fading opposite relation between them now.

The Vatican ruled medieval Europe. It took time and struggles for states to establish themselves as independent from the church. Even after the decline of the political power of the church, its influence over the affairs of states and certainly over the affairs of the faithful was and is strong. We still see remnants of this influence in things like usury laws. Usury was originally a church-defined religious matter and, incidentally, covered more business practices than simply interest on loans.

There are, of course, substantial chunks of the world today where religion rules to control the state as well as the minutest details of individual lives. Even in societies such as the United States, the power of religion is strong. Fortunately, most of us can ignore it, but not completely. Responsible political analysts attribute the G.W. Bush presidency's second life largely to the Catholic vote. This vote was gathered at the hands of a Catholic hierarchy out front in condemnation of John Kerry. Catholic or not, Kerry did not serve their needs. Fortunately, in 1960, the bishops either ignored or did not take a close look at the Kennedy brand of Catholicism. This was amusing in that at that time people like the great churchman and anti-Catholic Norman Vincent Peale warned against a Kennedy presidency as an invitation to the Vatican to run the country. The difference in 2004 was the kinship of Protestant fundamentalists with Catholic fundamentalists. This is a very strange soul brotherhood that could provide even more laughs in the future.

More striking was the unconscionable behavior of the president, Congress, the governor and legislature of the state of Florida, and the fundamentalists of all stripes, Protestant and Catholic, lay and religious, in the Terry Schiavo case. Thank God, and I mean that literally, that the founding fathers saw fit to provide the balance of the judiciary. The other branches were in league with some force other than God.

Religion is man's search for God. It is diverse. Unlike many of the cultural institutions over the world, its homogeneity is limited by the many different creeds and their mutations. The difficulties between

Christianity and Islam today are a sharp illustration. It is difficult for us to absorb the cooperation among various scholars in twelfth century Toledo translating the works of Aristotle under the sponsorship of the Archbishop Raymund. "It was his idea to create a translation center and to recruit the best scholars available to work there, whether they be Christian, Jew, Muslim, Latin, Greek, or Slav." (Rubenstein, 17). This effort was not just a happy public relations ecumenical gathering. These were brilliant scholars doing serious work without any censorship.

Governments, corporations, and schools grow more alike around the world as time moves on. Religions maintain their separate identities far more so than the aforementioned institutions. It is the source of much antagonism, cruelty, and terror, and always has been since Adam and Eve moved out of the garden.

A commonality in the midst of diversity of creeds is the moneypower continuum. If this could be harnessed into real theology, we would have a basis for complete ecumenism. There would be neither East nor West. It is a blessing to religion as much as to the corporation and government. It takes a lot of money to run a good religion.

For many years I went to daily Mass at a shrine. Despite my seeing the church as aesthetically unpleasant, it had one great advantage to me. After Mass was over in one of the chapels, I could go into the main church for real prayer and meditation. Almost always I was the only one there. Being alone with God in this cavernous, quiet space is a sweet setting for my purposes despite my dislike of its excessive décor. There seems to be an inexhaustible fund for the continual addition of buildings and religious sculptural artifacts at this shrine. Just about everything inside and outside the place has a donor's plaque on it.

About twenty years after I left the campus of the University of Pennsylvania as a graduate student and part-time instructor, I was back for a visit. With some time to kill, I went to the building where I once had my office for a nostalgic look. I was genuinely amazed to see that donor indicators, usually corporations, covered just about every square foot of surface except for the ceiling. The church I describe reminded me of that university building.

The turning point that sent me away from my daily prayer site for a time was a celebration of a significant anniversary of the shrine. It was a gathering that included, among others, a group of foreign cardinals and bishops about the size of a football team roster. An outdoor Mass

The Moneypower Continuum

was celebrated. A few days before the Mass, a table that was to be the altar was placed at the top of the steps. As I made my daily climb up the steps to go inside for my prayer, I had an opportunity to examine this altar. I am sure it was commissioned for this celebration. Outside a museum, I never saw anything like it. It was huge. It was graced with elaborate carving and intricate, multiple wood inlays. I have no claim to expertise, but I am reasonably certain that its cost could buy a modest house in many communities in our country. Throw in the matching lectern, and maybe a swimming pool in the backyard could be arranged.

I did not attend this holy circus, but, as usual, was at Mass the following day. I saw two tables under a temporary canopy. They each had a large paper sign taped to them. One said "Information," the other, "Masses." I don't know what the unit price for a Mass was. I'm certain the gross, which in this business is also the net, was overwhelming. When I climbed to the top of the stairs, I looked for ninety-five theses nailed to the huge doors by a contemporary Luther, but found not one.

Religion is pure myth. This is simultaneously its strength its and weakness. It is the strength of its genuine practitioners and the weakness of its superstitious communicants. The latter may be the large majority of religious people, and probably all religious people include some superstition in their psyches. But it is the superstitions that are the root of many problems. They are the basis for the moneypower continuum of the church. Historical uses of superstition by religious leaders as a means of controlling members of their sects are well known. Hellfires and excommunications, anathematizing and accusations of witchcraft—many devices have been and are used that have little to do with the core of religion. They are means for affecting some aspect of the moneypower continuum for the benefit of the leadership.

There is currently a particularly bizarre example of religious superstition around. Although Pope John Paul II ran on a very fast and loose track, dispensing beatifications and canonizations as forms of political patronage around the world, right at his home base in Italy, the people jumped ahead of him. They have canonized Benito Mussolini. Hundreds of petitions are left at his grave. They have the character of the kinds that are usually directed to saints or God. Requests for jobs, help with health problems, and similar petitions are written to

Mussolini. They have been compiled into the book *I Wrote to Mussolini*, by Robert Zollo. One hopes miracles don't start happening. Fascism is not what the world needs.

The root difficulty of religion as a force is the value of an anthropomorphic God. The true religious understanding of God is love—our love for God and God's love for us. We strive to become one with God through the medium of loving prayer. The anthropomorphic God is a useful educational device. As humans we need this device, especially in childhood. True believers of any faith should move away from the anthropomorphic images to the abstraction of divine love, to put the matter simply.

The anthropomorphic God is popular and psychologically uplifting. This is the god who promises wealth, good times, and many of the material goods we love. His darker side includes terror, warfare, and hatred. From the military conquests of Pope Julius II through the Holy Inquisition to suicide bombers and Jihads, this is the god who rules. These gods have no connection to God. Joined with numerous superstitions, they are the quintessence of the moneypower continuum in religion.

There are substantially less dramatic evidences of the continuum in religion. Numerous outright hucksters whose religions are merely vulgar businesses are abundant. They make their profits by scaring or by promising much to their hapless congregations. The more respectable and long-lived religions are not without their own pieces of the power and money games. Both their wealth and incomes are often considerable. They also really rely on the anthropomorphic God. They are somewhat subtler than the noisy huckster religions.

Just as corporations screw up, religions have been guilty of famous miscalculations along the way. Probably the worst marketing error ever made was the sale of indulgences by the Vatican. The consequences were as long lasting as any business decision short of destroying the firm.

Marketing anthropomorphic religion, as with the post-Vatican II Mass, is, I believe, another serious business strategy error. This modernization has not attracted many new communicants or increased attendance, which, on the contrary, continues to decline. I sometimes reflect on the possibility that the whole thing was a comedic error.

The last two chapters of Evelyn Underhill's *The Mystic Way,* under the topic "The Witness of the Liturgy," are "The Outer Mystery" and "The Inner Mystery." They are a description in detail of the mystical values of the Mass. It is beautiful reading, but as you go through it, you cannot imagine that anything approaching this description could be written about the contemporary Mass. Neither in substance nor mystery is there anything there.

A compelling description of the gap between the real love of God and the money and power of the Church concludes Sabatier's *The Road to Assisi.* This is a biography of St. Francis translated from the French by Jon W. Sweeney. The final paragraph of the book refers to the basilica to honor Francis, inspired by Pope Gregory IX:

Go and look at it—proud, rich, powerful—and then go down to Portiuncula, passing over to San Damiona, and hasten to the Carciari. You will understand the abyss that separates the ideal of Francis that separates him from that of the Pontiff who canonized him.

I have posited that there is a continuum among the four institutions as well as the moneypower continuum within each. Kevin Phillips's *American Theocracy* addresses with great skill the continuum of church state in the United States. Anyone who loves God and country should be deeply disturbed by his analysis. It shows with force the ugly misuse of what is mistakenly regarded as religion in equally ugly politics.

There are numerous quotations and descriptions of this literally unholy combination. My favorite is that by Senator James Imhofe:

"I don't believe there is a single issue we deal with in government that hasn't been dealt with in Scriptures" (96).

That statement is really scary.

In broader terms, Phillips describes the radical side of American religion as embracing "cultural antimodernism, war hawkishness, Armageddon prophecy" (100). As this affects politics, it is a wonderful set of reasons for irresponsible, unthinking policy, especially in foreign affairs. And it does affect politics and policy.

It is also clear that domestic policies are founded in a Calvinistic predestination mode. Markets will sort out the worthy, and the unworthy (the poor) need not be given any special consideration. Having been marked as saved by economic success, the godlike omniscience is another characteristic of the special people. Biblical quotation (perverted) guides them in all things. These quotations are given interpretation by their users. And why not? They are omniscient.

The most compelling denunciation of this politics/religion is its having no spirituality about it. Those who think that their hysterics of high emotion or speaking in tongues or other psychological disorders are religion, are sadly misinformed. These are only pseudospiritual effects, or spirituality at a level they would rail against, as it likely comes from a source other than God.

True spirituality is not exclusively a religious experience. The aesthetic spirituality of art is genuine and intense. But spirituality associated with religion is a sine qua non. The highest achievements of worship include spiritual experiences. Moreover the "religion" of fundamentalism lacks not only real spirituality but also an aesthetic. The sense of beauty is not there. It is ever present in true religion.

I think a few simple tests indicate that what is claimed as religious practice, and in some cases the whole body of the claimed religion, is not. They come down to whether the leadership acquires personal money or power by reason of their religious activities. They often promise the same to their congregants. This does not mean that wealthy or powerful people cannot be genuinely religious. If they are, their human achievements are not something they flaunt as fruit of their religion. Religion is an interior, private matter. They never use their beliefs as public methods of control of power or wealth. They never cite it as the cause of any material effect. This does not imply that those who are wealthy or otherwise famous who do not cite God as their source are religious. Some may not be aware of God at all.

From scriptures through the writings of the great religious mystics of all faiths, love of God, that is, true religion, is founded first on the virtue of humility. Apply that test to the most noteworthy of claimed religious leaders of all faiths in the United States, and the list would be nearly wiped out.

3

Academy

Education has a special place among the institutions wrapped in the continuum. There is no doubt that the problems of religious, political, and business organizations are becoming worse in our time and that the pitiful decline of education is both a cause of the present circumstances and an unfortunate foundation for despair of reform. In the first place, education has long ago abandoned teaching standards of ethical behavior. Concomitantly the reality of education has also been abandoned to the most primitive of exercises designed to make the students happy. They are not expected to think or work. They are not required to study any subject matter that might displease them, or much that does please them.

    The main purpose of education is to attempt to teach students how to win in the continuum game. Education prepares us for occupations. This is an accelerating trend in education at the higher levels. While a good school with a good student does have a deep effect on that student, it is largely aimed at success within the continuum. I can hardly be completely critical of this in the sense that we do need to make our ways in the material world. But the overly emphatic environment of education in this regard is unnecessary. Even more, it is misleading and robs students of some real educational opportunities. It biases their selection of courses toward the presumed enhancement of their continuum chances. I suppose that this was true in clerical education when the church dominated the academy. It does not have to be so today. It means not only that they are missing opportunities for intellectual enjoyment and growth, but it also deprives employers of better workers. We need people who can think and who regard it as important to do so. So it goes and continues. In the increasingly complex world, more intellectual power is needed. Educating or training students in soon-to-be outdated, if not already outdated, information and systems does not serve the future well. The difference between educating and training is inherent in recognizing the broadest understanding possible. Our colleges and universities are losing that.

Curricula in the sciences are no doubt more demanding intellectually. This is one reason why they have difficulty in attracting students.

Regardless of the intellectual rigor of the sciences, the courses they take outside the physical sciences taint the science majors as much as the other students who are there only to play. The behavior of practicing scientists of late attests generously to this. It is often on a par with that of corporate executives. Things like faked experimental results, the marketing of unsafe pharmaceuticals, and conflicts of interest between their financial and scientific interests are becoming as commonplace as backdating options in corporations. The formal institutions of the universities are complicit in these unfortunate events also. The activities in this community are well known to even the casual newspaper reader. There is undoubtedly much we do not know.

I think it is fair to note that grounds for the widespread cheating, lying, and stealing in most of the employments occupied by college graduates are one of the few definite results of the so-called college education. There has never been a serious study of cheating among college students that has not shown it to be widespread.

This problem of tuition being the purchase of a degree rather than an opportunity to become educated is increasingly acute, as there is little that colleges can do to train students for the continuous changes they face in the swirl of jobs in the international economy today. The academy must return to assisting students to become educated, so that they have the intellectual power to learn and relearn throughout life. Current efforts in this regard are not promising.

Despite the relative unimportance of church and academy, that is, compared with government and corporations, the two lesser institutions are as much infused with the continuum as the two greater ones. And therein lies their lesser status.

They are not usually very good at operating within the continuum rules, or not as good as government and corporations. Crudely stated, corporations are money and governments are power in their original circumstances. The continuum has changed this by blending money and power, but the ability to operate in the continuum is mainly to be found in government and corporations. True, church and academy can produce some real barracudas, but in the main they are inept. Their problem is that they must maintain a semblance of primarily serving their ostensible goals. Corporations and governments are equally burdened with these charades, but their goals are more compatible with the actuality of money and power. They cloak them with nobility, but it is a lesser nobility in that it is soundly wrapped with pursuit of money and power. Rah-rah notions such as Adam Smith's "invisible hand" and John Kennedy's "the art of the possible" fit nicely with real moneypower continuum. Church and academy cannot make it in the same way. Neither the search for God and salvation nor the beauties of cultivating intellects accord at all with the continuum, so the naked pursuit of money and power is slightly constrained. This does limit the all-out open pursuit, and there is no other way to do it well. Our two nobler institutions are somewhat hobbled in that way.

They have, nonetheless, adopted the business model as their regime. It is most interesting that not only have many governments and societies recently been reshaped from socialism to market economies, but also that all the internal institutions of traditional market economies have been swept along as well. They are all market institutions. Universal salvation is at hand.

Now let's go to the university. It has become a business indistinguishable from any other business operation, except that many of them do not do well. This too is a mirror of the larger market economy. At the top are the very wealthy, heavily endowed universities, who are the counterpart of the large corporations in the general marketplace. They are the General Electrics and Microsofts and Googles. Their power in the university market is similar to the big power corporations. They not only attract only those who they wish as members of the student body, and the big money from the supreme engine of the continuum, but they also set the required tone for the intellectual life of society. Much of what is perceived as intellectual achievement is largely a matter of style—not so much what is said and written but how it is said or written, and what are and are not appropriate subjects for consideration. Mountains of colossal waste are published every year, much coming from the top as well as from the rest of the academic marketplace. I note a serious comment in the *Philadelphia Inquirer* of December 15, 2005, "A professor at Cornell University's hotel school, having studied tipping habits for years and written numerous *scholarly papers* (my italics) on the subject." Tipping habits? How deep can university thinking get? Have they used up all the serious intellectual subjects? Sometimes I'll read a ridiculous recipe in the *New York Times Magazine* food section and conclude that the culinary establishment has finally run out of recipes. A similar reaction applies to studies in academia such as that cited here.

This is an obvious parallel with shoddy and useless goods and services produced by the corporate world. This is truly the main product of the academic market, certainly at the market leaders level. Perhaps the gold must be mined from low-density ores. Better, find ways to allow serious teachers and scholars to move their careers forward without simpleminded quantities of publishing.

The secondary product, sending educated men and women into the world, has deteriorated so badly that it is a wonder we survive. When Harvard dispatches a graduating class with 90 percent awarded honors, even the people from Nothing University can sense that something is amiss. Most universities are similarly kind to their students. Either we have been blessed in recent times with superintellects among the students, or grades are distributed like candy bars on Halloween. It is just trick and treat. The students know all the tricks, and their teachers give them the treats.

Let's go once more to the business model. How can customers be attracted to our school if they must earn their grades when our competitors are offering top grades just for paying tuition? (And often you and I are paying that tuition, via our governments.) This general reduction of quality likewise is a counterpart to much of the products of the other marketplace.

The second tier of the education market is composed of the state universities. They have marvelous resources, with slightly less market power than the top tier. They are illustrative of the counterpart corporations, whose fearless capitalism is based on government contracts obtained by various questionable political means, not by offering a superior product. There are many in the corporate market and many in the education market. The state universities seem to have a deeply felt and long-lasting effect on their graduates that is a wonder. Dear Old State is integral to their behavior forever. Their loyalties and proclamations of them in different ways go on through life. I expect that someday, if it is not so already, coffins will be available with the Dear Old State mascot embossed on them. (This jocular prediction was written well before the undertaking industry, or whatever euphemism it is called today, announced the availability of cremation urns just so designed.) No wonder that comedy has disappeared from our lives. Reality is just too funny.

Finally, we have the small academic businesses, in great numbers, that reflect the large number of small businesses in the conventional market. They struggle, as do their real business counterparts. Among all three levels the business model operates similarly. Heavy local newspaper ads are the key marketing strategy in these academic markets. Most of these are shocking. A graduate is pictured and his job is described. It is usually just an ordinary job. Why should anyone be impressed because somebody got a degree and then got a job of no special interest? Internet ads are becoming more common, but most of these are for e-mail ordered degrees.

Although it is easy to think of the second product of the academy as the courses and grades purchased by the student/customer, this is not the whole of the product. There is a package that includes enhancements that increase enrollments, but in the minds of some these are extras that they would rather not have. Just as to get something you want on an automobile, often you must buy a collection of things that you really do not want. The hidden packages of college tuition are a good piece of its cost.

Athletics is for almost all schools the primary marketing device. Alumni are encouraged to contribute by reason of the appeal of the team. Student customers are attracted to attend. Ain't education grand? Those athletic budgets are a nice piece of the base that tuition must support. Alumni magazines give lots of print, and especially pictures, for those alumni not too keen on words, on athletic achievements, however modest.

On its face, one would wonder if these rationales for the sports have any merit. The extensive expenditures in most colleges for sports activities would seem to be mutually canceling. Granted that it is a competitive game among schools to have attractive sports activities, there are a number of reasons that suggest it does not work. Winners and losers are not a consistent set. Sometimes schools have good teams, and sometimes they don't. Penn State and Notre Dame's glories ebb and flow for both students and alumni. On that basis, if the attraction of sports was as operative as is believed, enrollments and donations would conform to these cycles of winning and losing seasons. I doubt that they do.

It also seems illogical that there are not enough students and alumni who really don't become greatly excited about college sports. Wouldn't they choose their colleges and later donate to them for somewhat nobler reasons?

In a larger sense, if all, or most, schools are behaving about sports as indicated, then the winners and losers gain or lose practically nothing. Given other reasons why colleges attract students and alumni donations, and given the partially self-canceling nature of the activity, there are clear flaws in the reasoning of colleges about sports and their purposes.

Professor Frank of Cornell University has done some study on this topic and has examined other studies. Here is the conclusion from an abstract of his paper:

The findings reported in these studies are mixed, but the overall message is easily summarized: It is that if success in athletics does generate the indirect benefits in question, the effects are almost surely very small.

All schools have athletic halls of fame, with the annual induction of new members a large event and fund-raiser. I have never heard of a scholar's hall of fame. I believe that this relationship of athletics and scholarship sharply paints the nature of the business of education.

The role of athletics in attracting students and alumni donations is still another myth of no credence. Numerous studies have concluded that the claimed benefits are not attained or that the gains are of such small quantities that only the simple minded would continue to pursue them.

So who are the beneficiaries of college? The model says the students, just as the corporate model cites the customers. The actuality grants the rewards primarily to those in control, just as we have seen in religious organizations.

The bag is mixed regarding beneficiaries. The state universities may be operating for the athletic directors and coaches, especially in football. Many states are proud to have their coaches as the highest-paid state employees. In all academic markets the benefits accrue to the administrators of the university first. This is another keen parallel to the corporate management scheme. Bureaucracies of administration in colleges may be the fastest-growing employment group in the economy. In the city of Philadelphia, the University of Pennsylvania is the largest employer. Athletic departments are among the significant contributors to the grand bureaucracy, but those associated with nonathletic activities are also a huge force.

After the administration comes the faculty. Except for some superstars, faculties are regarded as wage slaves not to be taken too seriously unless they misbehave and get caught. This seems to be happening lately. Could this be influenced by the tacit understanding that colleges are simply workplaces, not centers of knowledge? This is not to say that there aren't faculty who long ago stopped teaching for various unhappy reasons. There are also many who are not expected to teach. Their customer base is outside the academy. It is usually more lucrative than the student customers, both for the faculty and the institution. This group is closer in alignment to the administration regarding beneficiaries. Their skills are successfully marketed to government and business, with larger rewards than those who merely sell their products to students. Aggressive pursuit of patents and other trappings of pure business establishments are common. Nobody even tries to maintain the I of genteel academia.

The least of all faculty are the large and growing group who mirror the business practice of outsourcing work abroad to gain labor services at horribly low wages. They are mostly domestically raised, but otherwise are like the outsourced workers. I mean, of course, the adjuncts. There is no rationale for their circumstances that could be considered ethical.

They get no benefits. They are paid something on the order of 60 percent of what the lowest-paid full-time faculty member is paid. The effect of no benefits is not included in that ratio.

Realistic conclusions on their circumstances are straightforward. Either they are inferior to the regular faculty, and that means the customers are being cheated, or they are as good as the regular faculty, and they are being cheated. The latter seems to be the case. Their resource use is an example of profit maximizing by cost reduction. They are, though, a sound example of a free labor market. There is little dearth in supply, thus wages are driven down. I never understood how this market is regarded as legal. Patent discrimination is at work here, but adjuncts are not a protected class, I suppose.

In the spirit of the times, here is another disclosure. I was a long-term adjunct professor. I loved it. I thought it was wonderful, and I gave it everything I had to offer. But I gradually realized that my self-delusion that my students were no different from those I had taught as a young man could no longer be sustained. I had to eventually recognize their indifference and genuine ignorance. The rewards of teaching were no longer there, so I gave it up. When I wrapped myself in the self-delusion, I was retired from an occupation that regarded its staffs more highly.

There is one matter of amusement about adjuncts where I taught. Faculty have to pay a modest parking fee. It's $100 for the year for full-time teachers, and $20 per semester for part-time teachers. Your vehicle must display your parking tag on faculty lots. Adjuncts get a different color tag from full-time faculty, and the tags are clearly labeled "adjunct." I cannot imagine what that is all about. Does it mean "unclean"? Or, if an adjunct professor parks illegally is he dealt with more harshly than a full-time person would be? It is one of those amusing little mysteries of academia—certainly not the only one.

As with any business, growth is a necessity. This is why we have such wonderful easygoing playgrounds for children in their late teens and early twenties. Growth requires attracting more customers. A business cannot treat its customers too shabbily. It must cater to them. So the academy provides athletics, high grades for course work, and other amenities not at all related to the purpose of the institution. One result of all this "education" is a postcollege society made up of children who never grow up.

The Moneypower Continuum

These chronological adults have been indoctrinated into a collection of devices and institutions that encourages, and they eagerly accept, living a never-ending childhood. Whether as participants or observers, games occupy many hours of their time each week. When neither watching nor playing, games are the staples of conversation, especially for men. In Pennsylvania, a governor devoted a large amount of public time to the Philadelphia Eagles. He has not ever caught on to what a hopeless task he undertakes. He has a sports commentary slot on a network owned by the cable company (Comcast) that dominates the city where he was once the mayor. I am sure that his abilities, when measured against the other candidates for the position, won him his network slot. I cannot imagine that the splendid organization that is Comcast would have it any other way.

Another example of a politician as a very public sports fan, and the folly of this fandom, is the former senior United States senator from Pennsylvania. He defended publicly the scandalous behavior of an Eagles player, going to the point of implying a look at federal law regarding antitrust violations. Fortunately, he was seen by even the stupidest of fans as a fool in this regard. He was not heard from again on this point. It would have been interesting to see how this jurisprudential approach would have played out had he followed through.

Then there are all the pitiful accoutrements of attempted youth maintenance that we pursue. We take various potions and drugs, many of which are useless and even harmful. Cosmetic surgery is as casually pursued as eating breakfast. "Cosmetic surgery" is another one of those euphemisms that replace a substantially more accurate one, plastic surgery. The face-lifts I've seen in pictures of famous people and those I've seen in person of not-so-famous people look like plastic doll faces. Then there is often the rest of the body, which does not match the face. It's as if the person was in a time machine that got shorted out when only the head was treated.

Perhaps breast and penis enlargements work out better. I have never seen either in the flesh, so to speak. I fully expect that I never will, certainly regarding the latter. If they are better than face-lifts, it's unfortunate for the beneficiaries that their trophies are normally covered up. But with the trends in public behavior, soon they may be able to show the world every day.

A powerful marketing device that arose about three decades back is the "university." "University" is a word bestowed on institutions with as great a frequency as the "artist" label is given to talentless individuals. Neither has much legitimacy. That schools once called "normal schools" are now universities says much about the system. A college becomes a university by meeting some minimum legal requirements and often does so simply to attach some prestige to the place. In the last three decades the number of universities created must be a substantial multiple of those created in all of the previous history of colleges in the United States. An assessment of the raw numbers would lead to the conclusion that we are a people of incredible intellectual growth. Does anybody outside the vested interests of the system think that is so?

Making a school a university has become the equal of the most used (and baseless) advertising in the regular marketplace—"new and improved!" Its effectiveness has worn out long ago. As with much advertising, it becomes necessary because everyone else is doing it.

I noted some years ago on a visit to the Erie, Pennsylvania, airport that it was named, "Erie International." It was a very small place. I was with the mayor and asked him about "international." He laughed as he told me that they had one flight per day to Toronto. That reminds me of how universities are created.

A university should be created about a collection of PhD-conferring graduate study disciplines that will be enhanced by the intellectual and administrative framework of the university form. It should not be inspired by setting up yet another MBA program, and maybe an MS in education together with some other fringe arrangements. Such a "university" is patently a device that is rootless.

This "university" movement is a strong indicator of the decline of serious education that we suffer. It is among the elements that have made education at all formal levels a mechanistic, unthinking series of exercises. The university is only a form of packaging.

The students at these universities behave in ways that also belie the meaning of the word. Socializing among students and faculty has always been regarded as a rich part of the educational experience. At its extreme, going to the "right" school is understood as more important than anything you might manage to learn as a student. For the ordinary run of us not at the right school, the socializing is a genuine part of the education. It is a time of life when human relations, combined with a new stage of personal freedom, are developed in the young person. It should be an unconscious education as the student goes along with the formal education activities and the activities outside the classroom.

Conversations between classes, walking to next classes, and informal talks with teachers before and after classes form part of the net of my meaning here. They are recollections of my own student days along with my early teaching days. Critics of distance learning or Internet courses point out that the student misses these, among other, social experiences. It is said that the Internet will never replace the traditional learning environment.

This may be so, but as I walked along the corridor of my classroom building between classes, a substantial number of moving or stationary students are speaking on cell phones. They may as well be anywhere as in this "socializing" college setting. Walking along campus yields similar observations. Some smaller numbers are connected to headphones coming from MP3s or iPods. It doesn't seem that Internet learning would leave much out.

I believe that it was Aldous Huxley who noted that most conversations are about criticism and complaint. Just listen sometime, especially to yourself, to verify this. The cell phone has greatly enlarged the reach of criticism and complaint. This happens to users regardless of their location, but it is another little poisoning element on campuses aside from those already noted.

Another dissocializing piece of the education plant is the now common teaching schedules. I once expressed my pleasure at seeing a colleague who I had not seen at all, well into the semester. She responded that she was a Tuesday-Thursday person, and I a Monday-Wednesday-Friday person as the reason for our not seeing each other. I was only an adjunct, so when schedules are arranged the low-hanging fruit has already been picked. This is fair enough. I surely didn't mind. While I don't see these schedules as a serious problem, they do reduce accessibility between faculty and students and among faculty members.

There are so many devices that collectively contrive to make the campus a place of indifference. But that's not at all different from the world. And isn't that what education is about? Oh, my!

I will only note briefly here the epidemic of cheating that infests colleges and the lower levels of schools. It is commonplace to the point that many students may not be even aware that they are doing something wrong. I had a colleague who would regularly check Internet sources for suspicious papers and often found them. I chose another route. I simply stopped giving term paper assignments. Papers that are well written by students who did not have the ability of a not-too-smart tenth-grader were not unusual, and I did not know really how to deal with them except to call the student a cheater. Because I couldn't prove this in most cases, I decided it wasn't worth giving the assignment. Then there were the honest writers who often caused much pain to me just by reading their work. I would have persevered in trying to get this important kind of work done by students, but it became clearly hopeless, as is most of the rest of the enterprise called education.

There are many Internet sources of papers on college cheating. One of the recurrent themes is that teachers overlook it because they do not want to jeopardize their popularity with the students. It doesn't take much imagination to project that thirst for popularity is reflected in grading. In their tepid defense, teachers probably can't be promoted or earn tenure unless they are beloved by the students who evaluate them each semester. Demanding teachers are not good for business.

Whenever I posted my grades, the e-mails that I received seemed typically to lament that the sender was expecting a B. This is regardless of their abysmal performance, and they know what they did up to the final examination. The mystery to me is the popularity of the expectation of the B grade. Why not go for the A? It is just as likely as the B. The various reasons advanced in these e-mails for why the grade should be higher served to confirm that my judgment on their abilities was correct. I am messing up their grade point average. They do not see why my inadequate teaching should result in their doing poorly. There have been some more fantastic reasons, but they are unbelievable unless you have been at the front of a college classroom.

In one way, a recent piece I read says as much as any other criticism that can be made. It seems that the parents of graduates enter into their job search in various appalling ways. They call prospective employers on behalf of their sons and daughters; they try to renegotiate salary offerings, and they try to convince employers to reconsider their rejected children. The list of unbelievable efforts expended by these parents goes on and on. Many schools and employers across the land were cited. I thought as I read about it that it surely must be an urban legend, but apparently it is not. (*Inquirer*, 5/6/07)

So, not only are these graduates uneducated, but they are pitiful wimps as well. More than that, it demonstrates that we have at least two generations of uneducated wimps running loose.

4

Students in Particular

I am not sure whether any or all of the things I have seen and noted are what form the student. I don't doubt the influence of the things I have addressed. These things happen during their college experience.

But before these children arrive at college they often have been set on sorry paths from their schools and from other forces. The sum of schools, television, general social attitudes, computer gaming, movies, and scant attention to books has contrived to make them completely confident of their belief in entitlement. It continues to astound me that students who are barely literate in general, and certainly not literate in economics, expect to get a grade of A or, as I noted, the characteristic B.

Some of this entitlement expectation comes, I think, from their experiences in previous schooling. The ladder of excuses begins at the earliest levels, where teachers believe that the kids are not getting proper support from parents. Next the high school teachers despair over the lack of preparation their charges got in the elementary levels. Finally, the college teachers wonder even more what was going on in high school. So they must compensate by moving them along just as their academic predecessors had to do.

Symbolically, I think the educational plant enters into it also. I recently went to an open house for a new high school of which I was an involuntary benefactor through my taxes. After about fifteen minutes of moving through the huge building, I asked my wife if they had thought of including any classrooms in this school. We had seen a grand esplanade of an entrance, two indoor Olympic-sized swimming pools, a workout room as well equipped as any high-priced private gym, a huge basketball gym, a cafeteria that was marvelous, a gorgeous theater, lovely locker rooms, restrooms with Corian-topped counters, and it just went on and on. To be fair, the library was quite good. The initial collection was excellent. There was room for substantial expansion. A computer room also was impressive, and no sane person could begrudge this vital element to students today. Eventually we discovered classrooms tucked in the far corners of the wings.

When I think of the rat hole that was my high school, which I loved, I wondered how this plush environment affects the students. I do not suggest that primitive schools should be the lot of kids today, even though many are. But what effect does this facility have on the psyches of its students? I think they expect luxury and privilege. They think that it should be given to them. They learn that the essentials of education are a minor consideration in their environment.

These marvelous physical plants are probably the fruits of the continuing miseducation of the decision makers and the moneypower continuum lodged locally. The school boards have been schooled themselves in the belief that good education comes from a great facility. The huge myth of the educational value of sports is prominent in their misunderstanding. Even were the athletic values true to their myths, the intensity and demands on the athletes are obscene. Moderation in sports—keeping the play and fairness values in—is as readily pursued as moderation in whisky drinking by the alcoholic. It is just another business designed to excite their inept elders.

School boards are another moneypower instrument, ludicrous as they may be in that respect. They build monuments to themselves, yet nobody knows who they are. They have access to unlimited funds through the most unfair tax instrument we have in our economy, real estate taxes. Their power is usually absolute, and they wrap it in the nonsense of ill-founded myths of education. Ultimately, they often do great harm in many dimensions. They do not serve education. They do not serve students. They do not serve the taxpayer. They serve themselves, as do all the people in the other places in the continuum.

Not too long after the palace of a high school I describe above was completed, the school board decided that the athletic fields should be done over by surfacing them with artificial turf. Artificial turf causes more physical damage to athletes and is substantially more expensive to maintain than natural turf. So whose interests were being served by this decision? The kids are subjected to potential physical harm. The taxpayers incur more costs. But the board can take pride in being on top of technology, no matter how harmful the effects may be.

I had a student once who was having difficulties with my course. We were discussing her problems. I pointed out that with a greater effort, she could reach for a B in the course. Had I groped her, I don't think I could have gotten a more shocked reaction. Despite the arithmetical impossibility of her earning an A at that point, there was no thought in her mind that she should not be given the A. Her attitude was by no means unusual.

The sad part about this student was that I was certain she was highly capable. No doubt she could have earned an A. She just did not realize from the beginning of my course that she really had to perform up to her ability.

At the lower end of performance are many who never study or show up much for class and/or are not blessed with high intelligence. Colleges allow them in because they generate revenue. They are not smart enough to understand the F grade as their reality. This may well be because the F, I suspect, is an endangered species. I was one of the few conservationists who kept it protected, as needed.

My most incredible student experience was one that I still find difficult to believe as I write about it. It happened after a lecture. A very pleasant young man told me that I may just as well be speaking Greek in class for all he could understand. After a little probing, I realized that he had a reading problem. He did not comprehend very well what he read. I suggested that the school had facilities that could help him. He said that would be unnecessary, because after my course he needed only one more to graduate. I think I managed to hold my facial musculature intact at that news, but his next bit undoubtedly caused some acid reflux within me. To divert myself from reaction,

I asked what the final course to round out his "education" was to be. Answer: Practice Teaching.

There is a little more to this tale. This man had a real vocation to be an automobile mechanic. Family and girlfriend pressures forced him to go to college. Unless he gets smart at some point and follows his real vocation, his life is likely to be unpleasant. Why do we make him think that an automobile mechanic is someone inferior to a teacher with a worthless degree who cannot read, or to a highly skilled teacher, or to any other honest occupation? How many more men and women are there who suffer from his fate? How many good and happy automobile mechanics are lost to us in this way? He also told me that it was the third time he had taken the course. God forgive me, I passed him. If he is condemned to teaching against his will, he's probably no worse at it than some of his peers.

While his case is extreme in my experience, there is no huge gulf between him and the student body in general, hence society, regarding literacy. As anyone knows, the instructor can choose between multiple-choice exams (remember, I speak here of college) and essay exams. Multiple-choice formats offer the advantage of unquestionable results and ease of grading. At least I thought the results were unquestionable until recently. While students do not question the results directly, they do pose objections to a low grade on a multiple-choice test. Their objections are generally of a nature that despite the evidence, they are surely worthy of something better. It's a primitive mysticism that I could never grasp.

There was a time when the disadvantage of multiple-choice tests to the teacher was the time needed to put the test together. Today, that is no problem. On my computer I am but a few mouse clicks to a treasure lode of multiple-choice questions thoughtfully presented by the writers of the textbook. I can thoughtlessly put together a test drawing on hundreds of questions in the electronic test bank.

Some disagree with me, but I think that a multiple choice for a college student is an insult, though I have never heard a student express the feeling of being offended by being given a multiple-choice exam. The students are similar to all those investors who are sure they are going to win. They are only gambling. The extent of the gambling is wide, I think. I would puzzle over how a student could get a dead wrong answer on a giveaway question, yet answer a far more difficult one correctly. I finally realized that it is because they have no knowledge. They often are merely making random selections.

I alternate between the two formats similar to the way I used to commute to work. I had reasonable choices between driving and taking the train. Over periods of months I would switch back and forth as my capacity for absorbing irritants from either within the vehicle or without would be strained.

I was shocked to read something about multiple-choice exams recently. The article was about a lawsuit won against a firm accused of plagiarizing questions from the bar examination administered uniformly to all aspiring lawyers. This firm prepares our lawyers to take the examination. I thought it amusing that the people who are presumably skilled in moving people into the huge tank of lawyers should not be skilled enough to win the case. The shocker came when I learned that the bar examination is made up of two hundred multiple-choice questions. That explains much about the profession. I do not ever want to know what physicians must do to pass their licensing examinations.

I have indicated my feelings about multiple choices. Essays offer other personal disadvantages. The minor disadvantages include challenges from students about their grades in the environment of the essay format. As I write this, yesterday was the day I turned in my final grades. Today, and I am certain within the next few days, my e-mail messages from students will be abundant. Many cannot understand my failure to recognize their genius with the expected right of an A.

More important, a personal problem I have with the essay format is the pain endured in reading them. It is not that their essays are weak or simply bad. It is that almost all of them have no idea of what an essay is. My casual guess is that I typically see maybe two of fifty students who can write an essay. The rest have no idea of what the form is.

I'll get maybe four or five sentences. It is a rare answer that consumes more than a single page of a blue book, unless the writer has very large handwriting. Grammar and style are not worth mentioning. As language is our medium of thinking, their inability to use it says some awful things. Students are no different from the rest of society. The ranks of commerce and other occupations are filled with these illiterates. It is no doubt the worst failure of our education system. I cannot imagine what the cost is to our economy.

I had been convincing myself for some years that my students were probably no different from students of my time or many that I had taught over the years. I told myself that I was just getting older. Then my last two sections of macroeconomics, though not intended to be my last when I started the semester, suddenly impressed me with the notion that finally the complete fruition of the decay of education had suddenly appeared in my lecture rooms. I know that this was not possible, but the performances were really severely bad. Perhaps my years of fooling myself about their parity with other students of the past was no longer working, for whatever reason. I awoke.

That semester began with the decision to go back to multiple-choice tests. I could no longer bear the agitation of their terrible writing. I also realized that I had been seriously inflating grades in the essay format. As their essays were usually devoid of communication, I'd look for a word or two that had some relationship to the answer and be satisfied. That's a bit of an exaggeration but not by much. It does give the flavor of the problem.

The multiple-choice tests revealed that most of them knew nothing of the subject. I also gave an optional essay question that floored me with some of the reactions. For example, I'd write, "Define the investment multiplier, and explain how it works." This is not an essay, only a definition with elaboration. I can still see the face of the student who looked at that question and said with exasperation that he could not handle that.

Unfortunately, I also read Haynes Johnson's *The Best of Times* during that semester. He cited surveys of college students' attitudes, work habits, and goals from surveys taken three decades apart. The surveys confirmed my understanding of what my students were, which I had been masking for years. While the students deserve the opprobrium of their lot, the institutions that tolerate and encourage them are equally to blame. This is what the market requires.

Johnson cites a difference in thirty years in college students' goals in education and life. Briefly, their views on the purpose of education shifted dramatically from developing a life philosophy thirty years ago to financial success today. There is little encouragement for substantial educational efforts. In fact, course requirements are watered down to be sure no one is too much challenged.

Among the findings of the UCLA survey results (Johnson, 492) between 1968 and 1998 were these:

- 82.5 percent in the earlier year saw developing a life philosophy as a reason for college education versus 40.8 percent looking for financial security; thirty years later, the ratios were approximately reversed.
- Interest in political affairs in 1999 by college freshman had fallen to 14 percent versus 25.9 percent in 1968.
- Only six-tenths of 1 percent of students in 1999 were interested in government careers; practically all are interested in business.

(It is possible that the disinterest in government careers is not simply related to just wanting to make money. Professionalism in many federal government civil service occupations has been declining since the Clinton administration, perhaps accelerating during the Bush years. The ranks of technically skilled staff have generally been replaced with people of general backgrounds, not particularly into the finer points of programs. The expertise is provided by outside contractors. This can be very dangerous to the public good. Think only of Iraq. Whether this is because too much in-house skill is not wanted or encouraged, or because of the lower intellectual quality of graduates is a question. It is probably partially related to the market myth. As we all know, private enterprise is next to God.)

The surveys corroborated my own observations of students that they are indifferent to learning, do not study, rarely to never read newspapers, regard class attendance as about as important as church attendance for most Americans, frequently come late, and wander in and out of class.

I had, as I indicated, tried to ignore these things, thinking that I was just aging, but the combination of reading Johnson's cited surveys and that strange group of students I had in my last effort overcame me. There is no joy in trying to teach people who are not interested in learning.

A chain of events solidified during my last semester of teaching. Perhaps it began before then with the astounding experience of the education major who could not read, as I related earlier. This might have been an unconscious influence on my ultimate decision. In retrospect, there were a number of things working on me. I am convinced that these things are not peculiarly associated with the school where I taught.

Here are some of the things that worked toward my despairing of teaching as a worthwhile effort:

- With the paucity of economics majors, I asked my department chairman why we could not attract more majors. I noted that we had students majoring in physics, and economics is surely not more difficult a subject than physics. I was told that the physics department was closed years ago.
- One day while walking to the parking lot with a colleague from the language department, I related my awkwardness in trying to use my college Spanish in Spain. I suggested that, nevertheless, foreign language study in college is important in contributing to general knowledge of language and in appreciation of other cultures. It was then that I learned that liberal arts majors no longer have to take a foreign language. I assume that nobody does except language majors.
- A not atypical attitude of students was shown by two of my final semester students. One missed about 90 percent of the classes, failed the first test dramatically, did not take the second test because he probably did not know we had one, but showed up for the final. I was going to tell him not to bother but decided to see what he possibly could do on the test. Also, as the students have severely limited reasoning powers, he probably would have tried to argue in favor of his taking the test. His score was worse than had he made a random selection of answers.

He also was an athlete. The school has an entirely phony system of checking up on its "student athletes." The questionnaire requires knowledge about the athlete's habits and performance that you would not be able to answer about your own children. One semester I realized that I had not returned the forms, and it was very late in the term, too late to submit them. There was no follow-up at all by the athletic department. They could claim they had this great system, which is worthless on its face and is merely a bureaucratic paper exercise. But with the aforementioned missing student, I sent an early note on the form saying that he was destined for failure. Nothing else was heard from the athletic department.

Another student sent an e-mail expressing her dismay at not getting the famous B I noted above that she was expecting. Out of a total of 115 points, she had accumulated fifty-five. I should note that despite their serious shortcomings as students, they really are very nice young people. Personally I enjoy them. They just don't get it.

The local newspaper ran a story about the glory of athletics regarding a student from another school. He and his teammates had skipped their graduation ceremony to participate in an athletic event. Missing graduation was of no importance to him. Our hero noted that what he would remember about college was this sports event. Imagine! He gives no credit to that wonderful course called Creative Littering, taught by that charming Professor A+.

Or consider the Princeton University professor who tearfully announced that university policy now limits the number of As she can give them. This was on the first day of class. She could have no idea of the performances of her students but knew she would not have enough As to distribute to them.

Regarding the two sections that seemed to be my worst and last, it had been my practice to send e-mail summaries of my lectures weekly for several years. Inevitably, some students would have problems with their addresses and not get my summaries. They would be upset, so if I could not resolve the problem, I would print out the material for them. These last two sections apparently did not notice that I sent these summaries.

One day I casually noted to a faculty colleague that I expected to have to give F grades to a large number of students that semester. He expressed surprise, if not dismay, that I failed students based on their academic merits. He indicated that some egregious behavior, such as never attending class, was the only basis for his failing students.

In a final grasp at justifying my continuing teaching, I remembered that this small school had a wonderful record of sending its economics majors on for graduate studies in economics. So on the last day of the semester I asked a colleague about how we were doing on that score. He is someone who knows about what every economics alumnus is doing. He mentioned only one former student who was in pursuit of a doctorate. I knew that student, and it had been about eight years since he had graduated. It was no surprise for me to remember that he was a foreign student. So this information symbolically sealed my decision that teaching was no longer worth much to me.

I did, unfortunately, return a few semesters later to take the courses that a former colleague could not teach because of illness. Difficult as it is to imagine, the students were even disgracefully worse.

My observations here are naturally drawn from the school where I taught. This is not to say that I think that this school is unique as regards educational failure. I am certain it is just another business model, as are thousands of other colleges in the United States. I have a friend who retired as the chair of a History Department of a university in New York City. I casually mentioned to him my decision not to teach anymore and gave my reasons. He responded that his retirement was partly motivated by the terrible students that he had encountered also.

As though to justify my decision on not teaching any longer, within a few days of my making it, the *New York Times* ran an item on the mysterious decline in SAT scores that nobody could explain. I could have explained, had they asked me. It was about the same time that Senator Clinton said that college students are lazy and uninformed. I thought of the day toward the end of the semester when I was explaining my position about corporations supplanting government in controlling our lives. I cited the visit of the head of state of China to the United States. He naturally met with President Bush, but I asked the class if they knew who was second on his list to visit here. No one knew it was Bill Gates. In exasperation, I asked if anyone reads a newspaper. Not one hand was raised!

These students leave college with no established work habits and little intellectual equipment. For a gang that has the grail of economic success as their hope, they seem to do everything that they can to miss it. (There is one quite serious possibility about success, especially business success. It's possible that a college degree has nothing to do with it.) The college bureaucracy substantially abets these students.

Neither intellectual nor ethical understanding has expanded, but the bureaucracy surely has. This is no coincidence.

Bureaucracies are stultifying. Organizational structures are necessary for any institution of any complexity, or at least for one that has many functions. An organization becomes a bureaucracy as it feeds on itself and has financial resources to expand its worker numbers. There are always reasons to expand. Any kind of perceived need can require additional staff. Needs are created. Often loss or severe deviation from purpose is a cause for bureaucracy, which then reinforces the bureaucracy. As the business model becomes increasingly entrenched in the academy, more people and structures are needed to conform to the model. It is a self-feeding mechanism. It is a cloudy substitute for honest activities and thinking. Sometimes it is merely fashion. Every respectable college has a "whatever," so we must have one too. I was intrigued when the school where I taught announced filling a new position called director of faculty development. Perhaps most colleges have this position. It interested me on several counts.

It has the ring of business about it. Most large businesses have staffs devoted to training and development of their employees. The business model of education is served by such a position. Also, as the employees learn little in college, it is necessary for the corporations to teach them something.

I have been at times curious about what seemed to me, among otherwise dedicated and knowledgeable faculty, an indifference toward or ignorance of subjects of which I thought every educated person should have some grasp. I think of theater, classical music, some general knowledge about things happening in the physical sciences, general literature, and the like. But I doubt that the director of faculty development could have any influence here. More to the point, I admit to possible great naiveté here, but it seems to me that college faculties should be capable, if any group is, of self-development. If the faculty members have no personal dedication to intellectual development, then there is even less hope for education than I imagined. Here also, directors of faculty development are unlikely to be effective.

Because of the low-level quality by any sensible measure of the typical student today, I wonder what kind of faculty will be attracted to teaching in the future. True teachers look for the rewards of both learning continually as they teach and of seeing students acquire and appreciate knowledge. Absent the student response, the rewards of the profession disappear, and it is impossible to expect the continual learning by the teacher as the courses are given.

Someone who visited the Schmidt's Brewery in Philadelphia told me this anecdote. As a college student he had worked there. His visit was many years later. Some of the old-timers were still there. They told him he would not like working there anymore. They complained that it was no longer a brewery, only a beer factory. I fear that if conditions in higher education go on as they are, there will be only college factories run by course workers.

The great problem of the state of affairs of our colleges is that we are destroying our middle class. Any society that goes anywhere worth going travels on the middle class. Broadly speaking, these are the college-educated people in modern times. The accountants, engineers, teachers, managers, lawyers, scientists, small-business people, and the whole array of professional ranks are this group. We still generate these titles in great numbers, but their talents are so diluted that they approach meaninglessness in a society that led the world in building these capacities.

I noted above that, given the condition of nearly complete deterioration of education, I wonder how we survive. I think there is no need to wonder any longer. In 2008 and entering into 2009 as I write this paragraph, we are into a horror of economic demise that will eventually prove to be more than we have ever seen. No one looks to its roots, but it is because we have several generations of college graduates who are close to worthless. Their well-founded reputation for dishonesty while they were in college is seen again in business and government as their immorality and ineptitude becomes public knowledge every day from one place to another. The regular reports of self-delusion as they look at what is happening testify to the playground atmosphere of what was to have been their educations. They have spent years of higher education learning little to nothing.

The upcoming and present economic events will undoubtedly do more harm to humanity than the worst terrorist attacks, including many deaths. There is no evidence that the root cause of the economic travails is recognized. We have finally come in the United States to paying for the horrible scandal of education, especially at the top, the colleges. As the United States is at the core of the difficulties, the entire world is suffering.

Colleges for many years have been entirely irresponsible regarding their obligation to create and sustain an environment for education. They happily hand out degrees to people who never should have been admitted to college. You pay your tuition, and you get a degree. It's a simplistic business model.

I am convinced that these failed academies are central components of the failure of the world economy. There is little education in classrooms. Education is unquestionably the heart of economic development. It is the most important contribution of all the other resources that make up the mix for economic development. This has been unquestionably proven. It is why China, India, and the other economies growing rapidly so prize it. Unfortunately, they do not have a sufficiently strong base or the ability to absorb the onslaught of our dismal failure.

We have sent out several generations of graduates who have no capacity for serious thought. They have no understanding of the relationship between effort and reward except for the trivial activities of athletics. They have a frequently demonstrated widespread capacity for cheating in college. They see a good grade as an entitlement. Grade escalation is the scourge of colleges and is the evidence of the worthless degree.

Furthermore, there are now enough college teachers who have gone through college who worked the system the same way their students do. They may not know that something is amiss.

We hear much lately about the destruction of the middle class. The middle class is essentially drawn from college graduates. While there have been forces outside the middle class that have done some damage to it, the middle class has committed suicide during waves of four-plus years in institutions of higher learning. They weren't smart enough to know what to do about their disappearance. They did it to themselves.

In the near future, we will be importing our middle class. We will do this directly with people seriously educated elsewhere. This will not work in the long run because as their home economies develop, the attraction of the declining United States will dim. We can and do virtually import the middle class through the great volume of foreign goods that we import. In international economics, resources can be substituted for people in international flows. We can import either goods, as we do, or import labor resources to produce those goods here. We import labor resources primarily for the lesser-income occupations. The high level of goods imported happens because we are no longer able to make much domestically. When the inevitable time comes when the rest of the world is unwilling to lend all the funds to support our obscene levels of consumption, the pain will finally be felt.

In 1956, Edward Denison did a splendid study on the sources of economic growth. His undisputed conclusion was that the greatest force in economic growth is education. Dated as that study is, there is little doubt that its conclusions still hold.

The relationships that arrange themselves into economic success for a society are those among technological advance, capital investment, and education. The core role of education is that it is both the source of innovation and technology and the source of the labor force able to use the new technology. Most of the important devices from technology that are in our lives today would be a complete mystery to an adult newly arrived in our world from, say, fifty to seventy-five years past. An airline pilot, truck driver, meteorologist, airline reservation clerk, military person assigned to a tank battalion, or almost any occupation that comes to mind requires a substantially higher level of knowledge than did most occupations a relatively short time ago. This will continue to be true in the future. Probably the pace will accelerate. Yet we are turning out clunks with worthless college degrees. It is, no doubt, our most serious problem. It is undoubtedly our most serious unrecognized problem, at least not recognized by enough people able to change the disastrous course.

I wonder why terrorists and other America-haters do not understand all of this. If they wish to see us brought down, they can simply stand by and allow us to do it to ourselves. We are right on track.

Recently, I have become aware of the extension of horrible writing to spoken language. It is not only debased by poor grammar and form but also by a real inability for people to make themselves understood phonetically. As I first began encountering it, I thought that aging had affected my hearing in a way that I did not notice, except for sometimes not understanding what someone was saying to me. One day I was with my daughter, and we approached someone who had to give us a simple direction. When the woman spoke, I thought, here we go again, and I looked at my daughter, who returned my look of puzzlement. My daughter repeated the question. We got a clearer answer the second time. This person was in a public place where she had to give this instruction many times daily. One would think she would have perfected this minimal skill. I have several students whose conversation is a mystery to me. There are others to whom I say something quite simple in form, but they do not seem to know how to respond.

Once as I left my classroom building, a male and a female student were in conversation walking behind me. He: "Me and her ate in Treetops last night." (My nasty thought here was that his kid should not be allowed on this campus except to cut grass or shovel snow.) He went on to say that the "her" had an organ that she made. His female companion of the moment said with a trace of trepidation and wonder, "Do you mean something with a keyboard?" He replied, "No, I said board game." This was another confirmation that ears about fifty years younger than mine suffer the same difficulty as mine do.

No doubt the schools are at the root of the problem. Recently e-mail and text-messaging have both been a potent influence on the written word, often reducing it to imbecility. We tout these forms of communication technology as advances in communication. In fact, they are causing a degeneration in communicating that is really a danger to progress for humanity.

I have a friend who suffered the death of his wife. She had a cousin who lived some distance away. She sent an e-mail note of condolence. Bad enough that, but it was written in the supremely illiterate style of e-mail.

I suppose this in turn affects spoken language. I suspect that television has been another contributor to the spoken stupidity, but I don't watch it much, so I cannot say. Where I taught was not a weak school regarding faculty and curriculum. I don't believe that the students are atypical of the general run of college students. If Harvard has 90 percent of a graduating class proudly being the recipients of honors at graduation, my students are just part of the silly game. When another Ivy League economics professor responds to students doing crossword puzzles during his lectures by including an economics crossword puzzle on an examination for extra credit, is there anything serious going on in the class?

Oh the wonderful world of extra credit. It is seen as an entitlement. It is a ticket to passing or getting a grade higher than earned.

Students do not understand the relationship between effort and reward except in sports. Contrary to the touted values for life that sports are supposed to confer, dishonesty and violence are its main lessons to both participants and fans. Nobody recognizes these lessons much because they have been ingrained into our insensibilities.

What we call higher education is the middle—and upper-class recreation time. The students think, "I am here; put me on the dean's list. With my degree, give me a good job." I wonder why so many of them never realize that many of them get jobs that were done competently by high school graduates in the past. But of course employers now require the degree. What for? It may be that high school graduates are incapable of performing the work that their forebears did.

We find, then, that the enterprise of education is cloaked in the noble purpose of expanding the consciousness of its students. This is a goal that very few students would voice if asked why they were there. As they are never taught that message, they do not know it. The administration and prominently the athletic department, small segments of the faculty, are the beneficiaries. Much of the enterprise is supported by unfairly low-paid labor. The students are almost an incidental, necessary as they are to underpin the rest of the structure. As their real role is as customer, they begin with the romantic illusions that attract them just like the Walmart greeter behaves. Once the sale is made, they shrivel into unimportance. They do become resurrected later. The Walmart greeter reemerges when annual fund drives are presented to the alumni. This is a genuine business enterprise.

Villanova University recently announced that it was going to change the name of its business school from the College of Commerce and Finance. In earlier lighthearted days it was known as the school of comics and frolics. The name change is proposed because the name was antiquated. Seems like an adequately descriptive name to me. Oh yes, the dean noted that the new name was to be determined by the highest bidder. Opening bids started at $30 million. The rewards of moving from antiquation are considerably greater than I could have imagined.

The education establishment in our society has become corrupt and monumentally wasteful. Corrupt in that it operates on a set of myths that is largely unrelated to any intellectual achievement; wasteful because of the huge amounts of money that it takes to get students from their earliest school years to the completion of college. Much of the money is squandered on diversions from the real path of education.

No recognition is given to the simple idea that no school educates anyone. We must educate ourselves. A school can, and should, be an environment that stimulates and assists us to become educated. The largest problems of education today are that there is little recognition of the limited influence that the institution has and that many of them seem to do their best to divert their charges from their educations. This is true at all levels. It seems to get worse as the student ascends the levels of schooling. By the time they reach college the idea of education is almost completely lost to them. It appears that the most genuine educational efforts are at the preschool and kindergarten levels. After that, the educational plant consists largely of devices that are supposed to cajole students into learning without their having to contribute much intellectual effort.

The field of artificial intelligence (AI) had originally as its objective to build machines that could "think." Many wonderful things have come out of the researches in AI, though I don't think that thinking machines have yet been constructed. Many expressed fear over the prospect of thinking machines, but a far worse effect has been experienced. The many devices that have come out of AI and related research have had the curious outcome of turning thinking humans into the machines that should help them expand their intellects. No matter how much they seem to learn from their computers, video devices of various media, iPods and whatever the next set of marvelous tricks is to be, they almost take on the character of these things. They may absorb material, but its nature is little different than it was when it rested on the hard drive, DVD, or wherever else. The sharp kids who amaze with their use of these artifacts are merely clever, for the most part. It is well known that many of these toys are laden with violence. The models of behavior for children that these media give to them are often harmful. They reinforce the violence and dishonesty that the sports immersion foments. There is no reflection, there is no worthy expansion of consciousness, and their humanity is but slightly enlarged. The unfounded fear of thinking machines is gone. It is supplanted by the too-stupid-to-be-fearful unthinking humans.

I saw an ad recently that sums it up, however stupid the thought is. It read, "iPod, therefore I am." How many student dolts would even know the source of the clever (?) paraphrase? Stupid as the statement is, there is a good deal of truth in it. The users of iPods and the other wonderful paraphernalia thoroughly identify with these devices. They are their lives. They are rarely unconnected from one or more of them, except during sleeping. I am not sure about the exception either. Stop and smell the roses? They don't know there are roses.

These devices that are often incorporated into the formal aspects of education are expensively wasteful, and that is their appeal. Teachers, administrators, school boards and boards of directors glory in the expenditures. Pitifully, they see these funds as firm evidence of educational achievement. We have several generations of people processed through this system. Their thoroughgoing paucity of education perpetuates itself into the system. Whether it is knowledge, love of God, family, high culture, or anything else, money speaks to its value in more than the simple economic sense.

Apart from the traditional formalities of what is seen as education, there are the substantial diversions. Clearly, athletics is central. It is also a great demander of economic resources, which go into budgets of all levels of schools. Does anybody think seriously that athletics is any longer a part of education? It should be, but it has long been something else. Even at the youngest ages apart from school, it is a grim business that grinds at children and families. I see young children on Sunday summer mornings engaged in playing baseball at seven o'clock. I don't know how much earlier than seven they started. Sports demand time and money, and, of course, again the money justifies. It is not the sports activities that justify the money, but the money that justifies the sport. There is little sport in sports. It is business, and often-nasty business and, more, harmful business. There are no games; there are contests aimed at hurting kids. It is a subtle form of child abuse.

Here is a comment by Warren Goldstein, chair of the History Department at the University of Hartford, on baseball. Its main ideas could apply to any professional sport. Much of its spirit applies to school sports as well. It appeared in a column he wrote for the *Philadelphia Inquirer*, January 16, 2007:

"Researching the game's early history, I thought I would discover genteel clubs in the world of the robber barons, green spaces in urban slums, honorable ideals standing against unrestrained greed. Instead I found a business like the other Gilded Age businesses: thieving, conniving owners seeking monopoly control; bosses picking players' wallets and fattening their own by using the reserve rule; political connections, blacklists and Pinkerton detectives; players organizing unions; managers playing nasty ethnic and racial politics; players who gambled, boozed, and threw games . . ."

This was written against the backdrop of the even uglier scandals of the sport today.

Consider only the amount of real estate devoted to sports at the average college campus or high school. Add in the equipment and staffing, and the size of the enterprise is enormous relative to the rest of the components of the educational plant, that is, those things that are really supposed to be engaged in learning.

They start with the "only thing," as one of its legends famously described it—winning. The total emphasis on winning clouds everything. It encourages any means to get there. Dishonesty and unwarranted physical harm either to the opponent or to the perpetrator are commonplace. Hurts also come in psychic doses.

The varieties of sports activities grow continually. Just one indicator of "new" sports can be gathered from the quadrennial Olympics and the new sports that come along each time. Television supports and magnifies the volume of sports activities and their audiences. It consumes many hours of broadcast time. More and more activities are named as sports and are shown, especially by the cable companies. Heavy, nonthinking devotion is the case for millions of people, mostly men, but with a growing interest by women as women's sports ascend. Consider one of the fastest growing "sports" in this great land of ours, NASCAR. I read a delightful description of its fans as being a mob of screaming, sewer-mouthed drunks . . . and their husbands. Sports activities are one definite human activity for which our educational institutional morass well prepares our population. It is a pity that the machinery of education is practically useless in providing thinkers, artists, and high levels of ethical human behavior.

I believe that there are few pockets of genuine education remaining at the college level. Students pursuing the arts, such as music or other art forms, are probably dedicated to their educations. This may be in part because a physical skill is needed. The techniques are definable and difficult to attain. Artistic achievement is only vaguely definable and is gained by a small portion of those trying.

I think that there is something of value to education in the requirements of the art student. It would be a splendid actuator of intellectual merit to include these combinations in education at large, especially at the college level. The only specific charge to do something physically during college is in sports participation. A limited, if growing, number of students are directly involved, and, for reasons I have cited, this contributes not much to education. There are several reasons for requiring some physical activity combined with associated intellectual endeavors from students.

We seem to have lost the understanding of the value of work in society. Everything possible is done with electronic devices or by hiring someone to do the job for us. We disconnect from the world about us in all ways possible. Doing some physical work not only connects us to our environment but also gives us opportunity to think as we do it, unrestrained by too many distractions. I have always gotten deep pleasure from cutting grass, whether riding on a tractor for hours on my farm or walking behind a mower on my suburban lawn. The mind floats free as the cut grass unfolds in patterns that please, and you are trapped in the task so you must do some thinking.

Some of this should be required of all college students in each year of their stay. They should have to acquire a skill of their choosing and write about what that skill gave them intellectually or spiritually or both. They need not attempt to become masters of the skill, but should be able to display some competence in its exercise. They could keep with it for all four years or change four or fewer times over their college careers.

The list of possibilities should be open but not frivolous. Learn carpentry or a musical instrument, maintain a collection of plants, learn ballroom dancing—any number of things could be selected from usually nonacademic pursuits that must involve some physical activity.

The connection to something real and occupying for the student in the suggested activities is only half of the benefit. The exercise of creativity that these activities should entail offers one of life's deep satisfactions. It does not take high levels of artistry or creativity to enjoy. It is a secret pleasure regardless of the achievement level. When

I play my tenor saxophone, it doesn't matter how badly I play. Nobody hears but God, my poor wife, and me. It is one of the good ways to pray, played in the right spirit.

More important is that the right-side brain dominance offers an intellectual exercise that tends to be neglected in formal education. This is brain activity that is powerful not only in its own right but that also bolsters intellectual power generally. No truly great mathematician or carpenter has achieved that greatness without the infusion of creativity into the art.

5

Government

Though the following comments refer primarily to the national government, most of what is said applies equally to all levels of government. Starting at the top, the presidency and many other elective offices are contests that are often decided by the amount of money that the candidates can gather. Each election becomes more and more expensive. The moneypower continuum is as sleekly fused into presidential campaigns as it is in any other place that we can find. The political fund-raising never ends for the incumbent as long as there is legislation to be designed for the good of the people. Lobbyists are well informed on the good of the people. They are also useful in seeing to funding of campaign expenditures. Their combined talents are significant forces in legislation and election campaigns. Early candidates drop out not necessarily because their messages are not being favored, but because their messages are already outvoted by the money that is in the hands of their political competition. Not only is our continuum powerful in this respect, but also it is the unbreakable link uniting the corporate and the governmental powers. We don't get the government we deserve; we get the government that they buy.

Why the power of money and its continuous escalation? The answer is simple; it started with television and has grown with the Internet. There is no other way to get elected. In fact, a refinement of the campaign budget is the importance of the television line item and the ability to buy large amounts of time. If this line item runs short, or is used unwisely, the candidate can die in the stretch.

The television establishment incorporates great power as a communications medium. It shapes public morals, thinking, and taste more forcefully than does any religious sect or educational institution. (Hence the appallingly low levels of morals, thinking, and taste, in which we take such pride.) Its ties to business and government and the public entitle it to be the quintessential medium of the continuum. Politicians must have it to get elected. Business needs it as its most powerful advertising tool. It is their most irrational medium. It generates little thought on politics or anything else. It is essentially mesmerizing, which makes it perfect for vote gathering.

It is largely responsible for the high levels of irrational consumption. It is regulated by organizations that are controlled by those who need it to get elected, and on and on it weaves through the fabric of everything in life. Corporations, governments, churches, and universities use and abuse it regularly. Its power is notable in that the average citizen/consumer is said to watch it eight hours per day. Whether from commercials or program content, the effect is strong.

And not much differentiates programs and advertising except for the louder sound volume at which commercials are thrown at the audience. I believe that programs and their advertisements are a seamless experience for the audience. The annual serious press attention to the winner of the Super Bowl of ads during the supremely "religious" experience of that football game attests to the unity of ad and program.

I will touch on the Internet briefly for now because it is still young and does not get the same attention that television does. But it is coming on strong even in politics. Its power is great and getting greater. Its capacity for generating immorality and genuine criminal insanity exceeds that of television in spectacular instances. Television is more generalized in these ways and is not as directly detectable as an influence in individual cases. Internet tracing of the insanities of its criminals is easier than connecting the nastiness of television to its inspired criminals.

Government offices, both appointed and elected, are important in the continuum—starting from the traditional political component and then enlarging into the money component. The only presidents in recent history who have left the presidency to return mainly to their pre-presidency modest lives have been Harry Truman and Jimmy Carter, the former more so than the latter. The presidency has a curious way of enriching those who attain it.

The continuum in government oscillates. That is, sometimes the moneypower forms by initially coming from regular politics moving to the money, and sometimes in the opposite direction. The Congress of the United States could well be renamed between its houses as the House of Representatives and the House of Millionaires, although the House of Representatives is not seriously lacking in monied members either. The Senate is a good study of the continuum's initiation from the money or from the power. Some of its members became millionaires after they acquired their power; others entered the Senate after they were first millionaires. Of the latter, some purchased their membership from mostly their own funds. Those who were first millionaires exhibit my thesis in that the money was incomplete. They needed to enhance the continuum. Half of a continuum is not better than none. In the purchased memberships, the need was a desperate one.

Senator Ted Stevens is a prime example of a senator who became a millionaire while attending to the people's business in the Senate but who apparently gave equal time for his own business, with outstanding results for himself. The *Los Angeles Times* describes his financial acumen in a December 18, 2003, article: "Stevens helped save a $450 million military housing contract for an Anchorage businessman. The same businessman made Stevens a partner in a series of real estate investments that turned the Senator's $50,000 stake into at least $750,000 in six years." Just the length of one Senate term is all it took. Many taxpayers could retire on that one little deal with due caution managing their money.

He also managed to get millions of dollars of defense contracts to a firm that pays $6 million yearly for a building lease that the senator has a stake in, according to the *Times*. Do not judge the senator too harshly. He is apparently a devoted husband and father. His wife earned tens of thousands of dollars on an inside deal with a company that benefitted from his legislative activities. His sons, sons-in-law, and brother-in-law all have enjoyed considerable earnings from his love of family as expressed by his influence in the Senate. I once worked for a political appointee administrator who, when questioned about the propriety of his or others' maneuvering federal money about, responded, "What are friends for?" Surely the senator knew what friends are for.

Stevens was generous well beyond family and friends. Indeed, he must touchingly see all of the people of Alaska as family and friends. Federal spending in his state is 70 percent above the national average measured per capita. This money was affectionately known as "Stevens money" locally.

Nor should we be unkind in thinking about Senator Stevens especially. His is a tale often told. Only the names and dollar amounts change.

We can look to his former esteemed colleague across the aisle, Senator Corzine for an example of the moneypower continuum exercised by someone who came into it from the millionaire first, politician later angle.

The *Bergen Record* of May 28, 2000, wrote: "Make no mistake about it, John Corzine is trying to buy his way into the United States Senate. Mr. Corzine is spending money, mostly his own, at alarming amounts in an effort to win his Democratic primary race." The spending for the race was $30 million, which was more than any other Senate race in history. His opponent, who lost, of course, spent $2 million.

His opponent for the governorship, unlike his senatorial opponent, also had millions of his own to spend. I suppose that we should be pleased that the money was more evenly matched than it was during his senatorial effort. Levitt and Dubner, in *Freakonomics,* challenge the idea that money is what wins elections. Whether their conclusions are correct does not matter. As with much of the mythology here and elsewhere in our lives, so long as it is believed that money is what counts most, the unholy combination of money and electoral politics will prevail. More and more political candidates are coming from the ranks of millionaires. This is not government by the people as I am inclined to see things.

We are approaching the ugly position in our politics at all levels that personal wealth plays more and more a role in campaigns. Millionaire versus millionaire is not an unusual picture of political races. It is hard to think of a more debilitating influence on democracy. This may be one of the reasons why a new order in our lives, domination by corporations, is happening. Personal wealth accumulated in one way or another through corporations means that the corporations themselves may as well take over, to put it crudely.

In some outstanding respects, they are the government. A powerful corporation was a substantial operator in the actual warfare in the war in Iraq. The supermess of the financial institutions of 2009 is another example. The point of the named war wager and financial groups is that they were beyond any significant control of the formal government. They did what pleased them.

Returning to our senator examples, the essence of the moneypower continuum over all else is indicated. The Republican, of the party supposedly reluctant to get involved with big spending, lavishly distributes taxpayers' money much better than just about anyone else of his peers of any political coloration. The Democrat, of the party of the people, gains his office by using personal resources much better than any of his peers on either side of the aisle (so far). Political philosophy, fiscal policy, and electoral fairness (that is, democracy), count for little. The moneypower continuum rules.

Appointees to government positions often are another set of players in the continuum. They too strike in two directions. Cabinet and subcabinet appointments may arise from various needs of the corporate continuum. A powerful corporation or trade group needs to have an on-site representative in government lest they be forced into the unthinkable arena of outright economic competition or be cudgeled with having to pay a fair share of taxes, or similar indignities. Champions of free enterprise have so long invested in the powers of government that here is another collapse point for the economy should this structure be eliminated suddenly. Their inside representatives are placed there by copious funding of political campaigns. Amazing versatility often comes from these masters of the universe who swing back and forth from the corporate moneypower continuum world to the governmental. Last year he ran a corporation; this year it's a war. This should not surprise us, as the realities of extracting rewards from either set of institutions involve the same skills of the continuum and those rewarded are the same people.

Aside from the continuum siphoning its due from either the corporation or government, there is absolutely no reason to believe that business management skills are smoothly transferable to genuine government. There is a wealth of current and past history to demonstrate quite the opposite. One of its smaller manifestations was something I learned in my experience. When a new appointee or career manager with a business background began by announcing that he or she was going to clean up the bureaucracy and establish good business practices, you knew what was coming. Soon they would be acting with all the skills of the least talented government bureaucrats. The really understanding appointees and career people prepared for damage control. Sometimes there was a good ending originating in the new bureaucrat. They would reform themselves and learn what government was all about.

Here also we can see the continuum threading through the institutions of government and religion. I noted previously the point with the church. As an additional poisoning influence on government, religion has been inserted, as Kevin Phillips has shown so effectively. The continuum in its basics infests religion; it infests politics, and the compounding, ungodly interstices of these things leaves us in a world of awful disarray.

Government has lately debased religion and politics in so many ways that there is little wonder that the corporation is taking over. Not that this is a benign reform movement. For the present, it is opportunity seized. True reform must be instituted. The movement into dominance of corporate power over the state is little different from the initial movement of the state into the first position, overtaking the church. It was hard to tell who the good guys were, or, more likely, if there were any. Eventually things got better.

As to the steep infusion of religion into politics and other aspects of our lives, Thomas Merton described the ugliness of this sacrilege long before it became as prominently engaged as it is now. He describes religious zeal as becoming political fanaticism whenever God is invoked for reasons having nothing to do with God. Aside from political fanaticism, he cites inappropriately invoking God to justify a social or economic system.

These thoughts are surely applicable to our circumstances today. Merton's book *Contemplative Prayer* was published in 1969.

The two dominating institutions of our lives, the corporation and government, sizzle with the moneypower continuum. For most of us their influence is overwhelming. No church, no school, comes near to their domain. For many of us, church has no influence whatever, but for those for whom it does, the influence is sociological or psychological, not really religious. We can see data showing a large number of us believe in God, but that belief is as affecting as our belief in the planets. (Of course, believers in astrology have infinite belief in the planets.) It doesn't have much to do with the way we live. The corporation and government have substantial effect on our lives every day. We can ignore God, as we usually do, but we cannot ignore government or the corporation. They shape every moment of our lives in some way.

6

The Corporation

It began as a simple device to affect trade and facilitate it by spreading the risk. It has grown beyond imagining and continues its growth. Growth in this case is not merely a matter of size. It includes functions and power.

The separation of ownership and control in the corporation has been recognized for a long time, as noted in Berle and Means. It has always been viewed as a problem. Ultimately, it rates a "tsk-tsk" then is shrugged off as unsolvable. There is also the continuing ingenuity of corporation managers, who devise new ways of sustaining and widening the chasm. Some solutions have been proposed and tried. (Probably the most compelling and intelligent set of solutions of late has been John Bogle's *The Battle for the Soul of Capitalism*.) This has been prompted by many of the things I address here. (More on Bogle later.)

We might consider socialism as one of the attempted solutions. Today there is not much room in the civilized(?) world for anything but market economies and, thus, the corporation. I have lately realized that the failure of socialism is associated with its ways of managing. It is government by committee. This often appears as democracy and may be so intended. Ultimately, committees, especially large numbers of them in one organization, atrophy. This has been the experience of socialism aside from the tyranny often associated with socialism in our times. Underlying the ineptitude of tyrants in socialism is the necessity for managing many committees. This failure path is often the base for the demise of the socialist tyrant, as well as other more political and social problems that erupt.

Even without the organizational problems in managing a socialist government, socialism is a system that would be effective only for a community of saints. There are no such communities, nor have there ever been. Capitalism requires a community of sinners. Sinners always win. (Nice guys don't.) Sinners are always not only more abundant than saints but also more popular. This is why capitalism ascends. It has been described as charged by the oxymoron "enlightened self-interest." There is not a college economics textbook that doesn't quote that one. It has become one of our basic truths. But enlightenment has dimmed with time, if ever it did shine.

Enlightened self-interest works something like this. A deregulated trucking industry permits just about anyone who can borrow enough money to buy a rig to enter and compete. As we well know, the holy grail of profit maximizing really drives that rig. The goal is attained by moving goods around the economy rapidly so the consumer benefits from lower costs. If the enlightened self-interest of the driver/owner pushes beyond the legally permitted driving time, and he falls asleep and rolls over on top of your car, this limits the benefits of the market economy. There seem to be a lot of rollovers since deregulation.

We can view enlightened self-interest as flag-waving terminology in several ways. The usual interpretation is that business aiming for its own purposes serves the public good. Jobs are created; good products are produced.

On its face, the term is a contradiction. Enlightened self-interest can only mean the enlightenment is for the benefit of the enlightened one. Incidentally, some good may come for others, but it is difficult to believe that the enlightened one is either really enlightened or gives much thought at all to others. This enlightenment can mean that thousands lose jobs or pension and health benefits. The enlightened were led by some spirit to underfund those pensions or load them with company stocks that offered little portfolio protection. This served the interests of the corporation but no one else. Enlightenment can produce shoddy or dangerous products. It does have unhappy effects on those other than its self-interested drivers. These are not rarities.

The language in its own right is dubious regarding the benign uses to which it has been put. It may be the business equivalent of the awful things that are and have been done to humanity in the name of the glory of God.

It is an anomaly that market systems now dominate the world economy in the name of free markets. The more powerful and the larger the corporation, the less the reality of markets that function freely, that is, as allocators by means of price mechanisms and competition. Even the pursuit of profit maximizing is doubtful.

Some will point to "competition" among huge corporations, citing the losses or actual demise of some at the hands of a superior corporation. This is not competition. It is economic warfare. That may not be too bad, certainly compared with political warfare, but it does not preclude the winner being the producer of inferior products. It also gives the survivor increased power. This is not the way market systems should work.

There is abundant evidence that corporate managers will enrich themselves in any way they can. Stock options, bonuses, and exorbitant salaries are becoming more the norm than the exception. Corporate accounting is larded with fraudulent devices to serve the bonus, salary, and stock options of the executives. Below outright fraud are legal devices that are devious and dishonest and that are sufficiently widespread as to discredit the notion of profit maximizing. And here I refer only to the many business stories that we know of. Surely, there are many that are unknown to any other than their sleazy perpetrators. Corporate management serves its insiders access to the continuum. Little else counts.

Describing the numerous infamous corporate scandals of the early 2000s, Levitt and Dubner address the problem of information asymmetry. The keepers of the gates are most interested in keeping information as asymmetrical as they can. This includes true information that is not made available to outsiders, as well as giving out information that is false. Consider Enron as a good example of the latter. (I might add that just about anyone who has bought a car is aware of asymmetrical information. The seller has a lot of information; the buyer has little. The seller is not above lying, either.)

It is fair to say that most serious business scandals are characterized by this information disparity.

Much of the ability to invest information with asymmetry is certainly related to the fantastic upsurge of means of dispersing or withholding information, as it shows up in every connection in this treatment of the continuum. All of the institutions of concern here are beneficiaries of this technology, for good or ill, and often the latter.

The widespread emergence of market economies is hardly unrelated to the power of the corporation. Corporations have not been given due recognition as motivators and instigators in the changed political configurations of formerly communist nations. This has not been politics in the manner of a regime change, however distinct the new form has been from its predecessor. It is not as though the Marxian forecast of the demise of capitalism succeeded by communism has happened in reverse. The environment of huge corporations and substantial world markets has been influential in the shifts from communism to capitalism. That is, the moneypower continuum is the motivation for the ascendancy of markets over socialism. Socialism just does not gather enough of the money ingredient in the continuum for enough insiders. Political power is another matter in socialism. It is comparable to the time when the church gradually had to yield to the state in Western civilization. It took a long time for the church to realize that it had been outplayed in the power field, and even in the moneypower continuum. We are similarly lacking in understanding the corporation in that continuum today.

Corporations need a large pond in which to grow. When they reach a mass in the nurturing culture, they subvert the social culture and take off beyond the serious control of government. It is transformed, with the moneypower continuum becoming the force within all of the institutions. It is perceived by all as the instrument, and the measure, of success.

A small example of cultural pollution is the stuff that is called pop culture today. The continuum has enlarged it, and the scruffy, horrendously noisy, vulgar, and ugly are the norm. Huge venues are required for presentation of this art to include as many high-priced ticket sales as possible.

Is it art? It may well be in that the definition of art is doing something well. In our time art is sacred. It is especially important as the sacred, because we have eliminated the sacred otherwise. Unfortunately, when we can be convinced that something is art, we regard it as validated in every other respect. So the pop culture music and associated artistic ventures are validated. We have forgotten that there are many horrors that can be artfully performed. Art is not an automatic validation of worth.

A large part of the public accepts the noisy, physically harmful and debasing pop culture in other forms. Let's not forget that public hangings and stake burnings were a form of happy entertainment in other times. (One hopes the hangings in Iraq as public entertainment are not the beginning of a new pop art format. It is certainly notable here that you didn't have to be there. Television gave it to the world.) Public acceptance is not a great test of a venture outside of the values of the continuum. Civilized institutions of culture are endangered and may disappear soon. Granted our educational institutions have abetted the process, as their business interests are also served by pop culture, but the corporate continuum is at the base.

A university offers a class in Art and Society. A newspaper article includes a picture of a guest lecturer in this class. From the photograph, at least, the lecturer is of indeterminable sex or even species; it looks somewhat like a large insect. Perhaps it's just a bad photo. It turns out it is a human. Moreover, it seems that it is a musician.

This musician contributed the knowledge to the students that art is not an answer; it is a question mark. Not a question, mind you, a question **mark,** was the quoted statement. That must surely be the most limiting definition of art ever contrived, and it most certainly was contrived. At least if it was defined as a question it would have had some utility to me personally. Those old highway billboards that said "Jesus is the answer," to which the inevitable scrawl of "What is the question?" was responded, would now be resolved for me.

So here we have a university attempting to educate its hapless students in what it thinks is art. A large corporation paid for this lecture as part of the subversion of art by the moneypower continuum.

Curiously, a week before, in connection with what appeared to be an attempt by this university to screw its faculty, it described itself as a "leading research institution in the country." For some reason this was seen as a basis for screwing the faculty. Its self-proclaimed superior status was seen as grounds for not granting faculty demands. Surely an institution that would host a badly presented lecture by this strange man on such a frivolous topic is suspect in its claim of being a leading research institution. Many strange things happen in our schools at all levels. It is also another evidence of power exercised by those really in control. Faculty, quaint as the notion may be, should be the university group most influential in the affairs of the school.

The market of the European Economic Union (EEU) was the primary medium for corporate growth in the late part of the twentieth century. The fragmented market setting that Europe was before the union kept too much competition in place. Just as the United States was fertile ground for huge corporations to prosper, the EEU has now copied the macrobusiness model of the United States. In fact, the EEU was intended to compete with the original model of the United States and has hopes of surpassing the original as a world moneypower continuum force. Undoubtedly, the further understanding of its supporting role in advancing the frontiers of the corporation will become a key to history.

Huge markets are the base from which corporations grow. There is little in cultures and their customs and history that corporations respect, beyond what is required to achieve their ends. It will be interesting to observe the rapid transition of the last large communist people taken over by the corporate continuum, well on its way now in China.

The most dominant corporations are very large and powerful. Here the continuum shifts decidedly from money toward power in its political sense. There is little that distinguishes the large corporation from a political unit such as a national government other than the absence of democratic or even regular processes that are found in some governments. Their revenues in many cases exceed the GDPs of most nations. Their power dwarfs that of most national governments. And it is wielded autocratically. The market is not much of a constraint; nor is government as reliable a control as it once was.

Numerous observations attest to the character of the corporation as described. Consider taxation, which is to the taxpayer an involuntary payment. Power pricing by corporations is in part an involuntary payment by the purchaser. Sometimes it is a hidden involuntary payment; sometimes it is quite obvious. How much influence does advertising have? The relentless and multisourced origins of ads that wash over us every day are as natural and deafly and blindly accepted as food and drink in our daily routines. What expenditures are done for the sake of fashion conformity? What choices in necessary consumption are available on the basis of price differences? What combinations of products are required to be purchased to get what we really want? These are somewhat more subtle involuntary payments, but they contain much of the character of being involuntary. I don't believe that most of us realize the extent of exposure to advertising that we experience every day. And it continues to grow as new media and variations on the old come along.

So there is much coerced expenditure in the economy, and this is not market determination, as the mythical market long gone would function. It is not even close. However, it does elevate the level of the moneypower continuum for those in control in the corporation. The power has shifted from the market institution to the organizational invention of the corporation. That is a really large difference.

Markets originated in human relationships somewhat akin to other common ways in which people related to one another. They were human. Shifting to the mostly dehumanized corporation marks a large change in what we are. At this point I do not mean to ignore certain beneficial necessities of this change. I'll look to that later.

The core notion, which is not given sufficient understanding, is that the corporation and the resultant changes that affect us are not simply an extension of the more human institution of markets. It is another world and one that continues to become still other worlds. There is nothing else like it in our age. Church and state remain much the same as in their origins, at least relative to the corporation's spinning into infinite space. They do change. Church adapts to new needs or opportunities but usually does so at a very slow pace. State likewise changes, but again it is usually not a rapid pace unless by revolution. And revolutions usually are a long time cooking before they are ready. Church and state are completely outpaced in influence by the corporation. The incredible ability of the corporation to change substantially and quickly gives it an advantage that is untouchable. It may be that the corporation as an artificial legal person is not bound by history and tradition nearly as much as are state and church. The academy is also highly flexible despite the supposed grand traditions of its environment because it is practically owned by the corporation.

This fluidity that marks the corporation offers us prospects for either considerable good or evil, and we see both.

The corporation is a political institution. It does not pass laws; it sees to it that they are passed to serve its interests. It does not raise armies; it lucratively provides the equipment that they need and looks to armies to protect its assets. Perhaps the most pristine continuum activities are observable in these kinds of activities. Infinite subtleties wrap around other things that corporations do. It has become a political entity in the way that it functions as well. Its myth of markets is useful but is pure myth.

So the moneypower continuum is cleanly represented in the corporation. The moneypower accruing to those in control is far more important than is power over the consumer. With the power to control prices and allocations, there are benefits to be distributed. Potential beneficiaries are the consumers of the products, the stockholders in the corporation, and the employees, managers, and executives of the corporation. Actually, all benefit in general from the present floating arrangements that are the corporation. The problem is that the increasingly major beneficiaries are the executives. Often their benefits are entirely unrelated to their abilities and performance. Even when they are, there are incredible excesses that clearly illustrate the key idea in the continuum that those in control are the major winners in this institution, as in others.

The benefits to consumers are not to be denied. An incredible, ever increasing, and changing array of products in advanced economies can make life luxurious. It also makes it quite wasteful. There are numerous evidences of this in the United States and other economies. The modern phenomenon of "shopping" illustrates. Consumers in large numbers move out into the shopping centers (an interesting name in itself—not markets), just to shop. They have no designated list of goods to purchase; they shop mindlessly. The *Philadelphia Inquirer* of December 15, 2005, offers this advice about the holy seasons of multicultural, multireligion, multiethnic, and multimulti (their nonwords, but cute), "If you want to be happy in a million ways, for the holidays go out and shop and splurge—on new outfits for yourself." (The awkward punctuation is theirs also.) The punctuation is forgivable. The thought is not.

Sadly, these victims of shopping do not get their happiness. Ann Satherthwaite, in her *Going Shopping*, says, "Yet the shopper's instinctive hopes and fantasies, though manipulated by overt advertising and covert persuading, are rarely realized. In fact it is that gap between the hope and reality that continues to drive modern consumerism" (123).

Shoppers are not taking care of needs; it is a purely social phenomenon. These are not necessarily higher-income people. Kmart and Walmart are well populated with the freelance shopper. During the slowdown of the economy in the early 2000s a Walmart manager noted with dismay that there were increasing numbers of items found in the store that were just placed casually on the shelves, indicating that shoppers were changing their minds about purchases and were removing items from their carts. This meant that they were actually calculating the amount they were spending! Apparently, this is not the usual way of shopping. Not only do shoppers arrive with no particular purchases in mind, but they also do not know what they are spending until they slip the plastic through the slot.

A key and troublesome aspect of capitalism that is reflected in the ever-changing corporation, and its continuum, has been the conversion of capitalism from a production to consumer capitalism. As we shall see below from John Bogle, it also has changed from owner capitalism to manager capitalism. This is an ugly combination of incredible change. It is the grossest manifestation of the continuum. It is likewise a tribute to the total flexibility of the corporation.

It is remarkable how the corporation has gone so deeply astray. It is very reminiscent of the Vatican in the Middle Ages. The moneypower continuum has switched from God to man.

The foundation of both capitalism and the corporation in its early modern form was with the railroads in the early nineteenth century in the United States. From there the economy became the most productive economic force in the world. During the post World War II period, the beginnings of the shift to consumer capitalism took place. Together with the awful devaluation of education noted above, we have sapped the economy of much of its strength. The consequences may be severe. By 2005, the economy actually had a negative savings rate. This is extraordinary for a high or even the highest-level income economy in the world. A casual stroll through an electronics store or a clothing store will show how little we manufacture in this economy.

Consumer capitalism, carried to the absurd lengths that we have, is a weak foundation for the future. We not only are existing in consumer capitalism by nature of our intensity of devotion to consumption but by reason of our doing almost nothing else. We make so little of what we consume.

Consumer behavior in light of Leach and Satherthwaite may well be analyzed as theater. At the end of 2005, Gap, a clothing retailer, after a bad year, announced that it was going to redesign its stores. There was no implication for addressing what we would call rational consumer behavior. Product pricing, quality improvements, nothing along those lines, was to be considered. It was a matter of stage sets. It got worse. The Sunday *New York Times* of July 16, 2006, has a front-page story in the Arts and Leisure section on the Gap's new commercials featuring dancers trained by choreographers of some fame in the world of dance. This story consumes about 2 percent of page one and all of page 11. Are we having art yet?

Around that time, the *Times* was attacked by President Bush and all good mindless patriots for publishing some facts about security matters. I am certain that this outrage of whoring the dance, and what used to be a serious paper dealing with the arts, will not attract much, if any, consternation. We have long lost the ability to distinguish between art for its own sake and advertising. It might be said that this is a marvelous integration of art into everyday life, but consider its tawdry objectives. That point is not a good one. Consumer capitalism shines through everything.

Store or consumer stage redesign is not unusual. Supermarkets seem to be in continual redesign. Practically all stores provide sound tracks as in movies. Few people realize the influence on their movie experiences that sound tracks exert. I sometimes am surprised to see sound tracks on sale for movies that I never noticed had one. My ignorance is probably an indication that the track did a very good job of being part of the film art.

Some stores that traditionally did not provide shopping carts have discovered that if they provide carts, people purchase more. Aisles in these stores were not designed to handle carts, so the atmosphere is unpleasant. Regardless of the messy place that carts make of stores, they go in. No one seems to mind. They do provide another opportunity for rude behavior. Movie theaters make their profits on popcorn. In so many enterprises, prices, values, and the merchandise itself are secondary. A contrived atmosphere to induce spending is the aim.

The Gap, Abercrombie and Fitch, and Macy's are all fantasy environments. They are akin to theaters.

For many stores there are two stages. The store windows make up the first of these stages. They serve the same purpose as the posters that are on the fronts of movie and stage theaters, but they are much more elaborate. They are prepared and designed with great care and are very expensive. Window dressing is a trade that can be generously paid. It is an occupation that originated with the first large department stores.

The window theater is an enticement to enter the main theater. Sometimes it functions as pure theater. I am certain that many people who are entertained by the Saks Fifth Avenue or Bloomingdales windows in Manhattan would be persuaded to enter and buy were it not for personal economic limitations. For them, it is simply theater.

A really calculated theater piece is found in a new-car showroom. It is something of theater of the absurd. There may be people who enjoy the game of buying a new car, but I am not one of them. I think I might have bought two or maybe three more new cars than I have over my lifetime were it not for the annoyance of the experience. I always put it off until I decide I must go through with it.

I conclude that the powerful corporation "benefits" the consumer mainly through a wide array of products that can be purchased without thought as to the products or their prices. If consumers suddenly, with thoughtful consideration, decided to buy mostly what they needed, world economic chaos would result. There are definite benefits to this nonsystem. Those who point out the disadvantages are seen as cranks. Enjoy! That is not my concern here. Can it be that consumers are guided by instinctive realizations that as markets are only mythical constructions, then there is no place for rational consumer decisions? Why should they play their role if the merchants do not play theirs? Merchants do not offer quality merchandise whose pricing is guided by rational market forces from the supply side of the market. The sellers build an arrangement of inducement far from the rational grounds for consumer purchases, that is, the textbook claims that product demand is determined by prices, incomes, and tastes. Prices are intact but sometimes are confusing. Incomes are undermined by credit cards. And "tastes" are shamelessly manipulated.

After the consumers and their relationship with the corporation, the next are the stockholders. They are involved in an equally irrational relationship, if only seen in their entirely opposite position from that of their ephemeral ownership rights. (See Berle and Means, cited above.) Rarely do the stockholders have any specific influence in the affairs of the corporation. They do have an overriding but vague effect on corporate objectives. The real controllers of the corporation must attain an acceptable valuation of the shares in the market, if possible, so as to realize their other objectives. With the increased importance of corporation executive shareholders and their stock options, the stock valuations become an incestuous objective even further removed from the interests of the outside shareholders. The results of these activities are as harmful to the institution as incest in real life to the biological stock. The outside stockholders may realize short-term gains but soon will reap the pain.

Many of the devices used to reach this goal have nothing to do with making and selling a good product that will, through high levels of sales, be reflected in the stock price. Neither the products nor financial markets that envelop them function as markets but as political devices linked to the corporate moneypower continuum.

This can lead to actions and policies that are quite the opposite of what the management myths embedded in the market myth would suggest. It works against the stockholders' interests. Quickly listing some of the problems to be elaborated upon later, there is a likelihood for expediency to prevail over long-term profits, for complex accounting systems often just inside the line of legality but over the line for ethics; and for temptation to fraud often yielded to. In other words, fooling the market and the stockholders is integral to management actions.

Contemporary circumstances for stockholders are made worse because of the perceived necessity of owning equity securities for retirement that has spread among many more families than ever before. The company pension plan is not what it used to be. The Social Security program was once scheduled by the Bush administration to be converted to a disgraceful set of problems for retirees. If there is such a thing as a sophisticated investor, their ranks are thin and become relatively thinner and thinner as the ownership of securities grows.

John Maynard Keynes called the stock market "gambling." It undoubtedly is for most of its participants. The only informed investors are the manipulators. (Keynes applied his economic genius in part to becoming very wealthy by trading government securities. No gambler, he. I have read a plausible account of his really avoiding gambling or risk. He did so well in the government securities market using insider information as a highly placed official in the Exchequer. When I was in graduate school, references to Keynes in textbooks and papers, especially those from England, always parenthetically referred to him as "the late Lord." Lord!

The realistic understanding of securities markets as gambling is further clouded by the advisors to investors. Most investors are guided by market analysts, who usually are grand examples of people pretending to have knowledge that is impossible to have. I sometimes amuse myself by reading these analyses with some care. They are very creative. This is not a criticism of the analysts. It has been commonplace for the style of their work. This is not far removed from academic or even any publishable writing style today that must be positive or assertive without regard to exceptions. Don't clutter work with details that might detract from your being perceived as a genius. Rarely does anyone read the financial analysts with a critical eye. We want to hear the good or bad, because we don't know otherwise how to invest.

A second category of analyst is more straightforward, with the use of verbal hedges so extensive that in the end nothing useful is ever actually said. This is another reading exercise to entertain.

The third kind of analyst is the super liar, who attains celebrity by the use of fearless recommendations that they know are as dishonest as Beelzebub. They are uncommon thieves, seeming to be unaware of ethics or morals.

Another problem that investors must face is the various manipulations of data that are commonplace in corporate accounting. Some of it is blatant and illegal. Other data are just this side of ethical but are misleading. Finally, there are the large "mistakes" that are made with some frequency. Evidences of these problems are in the usual restatements of accounts that appear in the financial and general press from time to time. These restatements can also exhibit financial whoredom. Unfortunately, these are not rarities. So we see restatements that change profits from three years back into losses. In this fantasy world of corporate accounting, stock gains were accumulated on worthless information, and then losses were incurred by the later stockholders.

All of this has nothing to do with the realities of profits and losses in the fundamental sense of producing real economic goods and services yielding profits. It is all part of the arsenal of the true beneficiaries of corporate largesse.

We call our system a market system that is motivated by profits. Neither with regard to the product markets nor the financial markets that play such a crucial role in business management do we have markets as we would like to understand them. Given the complexities and manipulations of accounting data, it is equally true that profits are an ephemeral and often unknowable goal of the system. Profits are what the corporate spokesperson says they are.

The market economy is a political organization that is not at all like a market system with a profit objective. It is operated for the benefit of the people in control. It has become increasingly elitist. It is a wonder that we continue to allow these things to happen. It may be that we have also allowed political scandal to be open and ignored regarding the formal political institutions of our society. So as we inherently perceive the political similarities of business and government, we ignore the terrible behavior of business and government. The moneypower continuum carries them both along.

Beyond the cited problems with markets is the more subtle difficulty that markets have suffered a dilution of their function as information systems. This is a very important purpose for markets to perform. Here I speak to the interrelations among different and all markets. The market system is supposed to be a general equilibrium system. Information is transmitted via the price system. In its most abstract understanding, the price of anything affects the price of everything else. This is the economics equivalent to the better-known idea of the butterfly flapping its wings in Japan and the eventuation of a hurricane in the North Atlantic.

The French economist Leon Walras first described the set of equations demonstrating general equilibrium in his *Elements of Pure Economics*. In less-complex ways of looking at it, we can envision easily that the price of our subsidies for wheat in the United States is going to have an effect on food throughout the world. Or, when consumers occasionally realize the interest rates on credit card balances they are carrying could extend the payments beyond their life expectancies, they back off—usually too late.

When markets lose their power to send this information, then economic confusion, and worse, ensues. The world has been increasingly denaturing this information with the tremendous rise of the moneypower continuum of the global corporation. While we can see the folly of claims of the market economy adopted by more political systems as though it were a true market system, the loss of its critical information transmission mechanisms is subtler. Indeed, those most famous for developing information systems are those most destructive of the information of which I speak. Think only of the power of Microsoft. Or think of the preposterous extensions of information monopolies of another important character granted by our moneypower Congress to Mickey, that cute little mouse. The patent office and its binge in granting monopolies for trivial intellectual property claims is yet another evidence. (Though the patent office became so outrageous in this respect that they had to calm down and stop their nonsense.)

It is certainly the very essence of monopoly to restrict information flows to its best ability. This is an ancient condition. But here again, the means, scope, and power now available have never been approached in previous times. Their growth exceeds that other scourge of humanity we choose to ignore, population growth. We see today the numerous problems of immigrants to various places better than those from which they came. It is easily explained by population pressures. There is no reason for this. Population control is available. The church and others foolishly oppose it. Perhaps if various peoples who have no other place to go overran the Vatican, there might be a different ex cathedra statement on birth control.

Surely it is difficult to speak to the results of these problems. Some signals are apparent. We can cloak the world, regional, or local economies in Nobel-winning equations about the economy, but we know less and less about its workings. Serious malfunctions may be uncontrollable by amateur institutions like central banks. Fiscal policy is so engrossed in the moneypower continuum as to be useless if needed. We need to think seriously about the future of the world.

Recent economic history suggests some of the problems of the disconnects mentioned.

A lag in employment in the midst of an apparent recovery in the economy in other particulars is not unusual. As economic recovery begins, there is always some hesitance by employers to hire more people until they are convinced that the recovery is solid. Existing resources are stretched until the decision is made that it is time to expand.

The unusual slowness of the recovery in employment in the 2003–04 period, when there were other indicators of general recovery, may have been partly ascribable to the information flaws noted just above. Some of the reasons given were excess capacity from earlier investment and sharp increases in productivity. What is not said is that the tax law changes combined with the sea change in corporate behavior may be the most potent influence on lagging employment. Maybe it has not been the case that the tax changes have exerted much influence thus far, but their potential for holding back employment is large.

Corporate management behavior has been sufficient to retard employment growth on its own in recent years. That corporations seek to maximize profits with a view beyond tomorrow is an idea increasingly open to challenge. Even if appropriate actions related to long—and short-term profits are still the case for many and even most businesses, the idea of stock value maximizing in a vacuum not related to the basic business activities is clearly the pursuit of a sufficient number to be significant. It also breeds and spreads as others are forced to play the game for survival. Profit maximizing in its genuine sense would be expected to lead to high stock valuations by the market. But there are a number of devices available to maximize equity values while disregarding profit maximizing and even jeopardizing it. They are often used.

They are also encouraged by the new tax provisions regarding dividends and capital gains. The tax reductions may stimulate the economy but not the sector relating to employment. Here they can have the opposite effect.

The tax rate now applied to dividends is 15 percent, as is the rate applied to capital gains. A dividend payment to someone in the 36 percent tax bracket is now worth substantially more than it was before the tax changes. Taxpayers able to influence dividend payments are practically all in the 36 percent bracket.

A capital gain also is now worth more than it was in the old tax structure. As both dividends and capital gains are taxed at the same rate, the preference for one or the other is somewhat diminished. It is still conceivable that a preference for capital gains remains for some taxpayers because it is deferred taxation. Clearly the preference is unlikely to be as strong generally as it sometimes was before.

Given these tax circumstances, advantages to the business community are considerable and are inimical to employment increases. Worse, they are incentives to decrease employment. High payments of dividends translate into higher equity values, unless the market sees through a ploy or a weak foundation for the payments. There is, then, a compound incentive for dividend payment increases.

Under the usual rubric of these relationships, this is the way that enlightened self-interest pushing for profit maximizing is supposed to work. The difficulty in the present circumstances is that numerous profit maximizing activities involve massive fraud, serious juggling of the data, and various other devices to indicate growth and profits that are spurious.

Aside from these irregular activities, achieving dividend payouts and capital gains often means cost reduction, no matter how ill advised these reduction methods may be. It is management in the Louis XVI way.

The principle mechanism is staff reductions. With the higher value of dividends, an incentive is created to pay them. One source of dividends is current earnings or cash flow. One way to swell the cash flow is to reduce expenses. Good management normally achieves success by increasing sales and introducing good new products, and only secondarily by reducing costs. Management today seems to prefer the easy option of reducing costs. This is a sterile way to show a profit. It is not always an improperly motivated action. Organizations do become fat.

It does raise suspicions, and often is a pitiful device to attempt to save some management skin or to enhance the standing of management regardless of business or ethical soundness. Some genuine psychopaths have devastated good companies with super employment slashing. Cheers resound when a major corporation announces a large staff reduction unless the company is known to be a mad cow downer. The cheers quickly translate into an uptick of the equity value of the stock. This activity becomes much more desirable with the new tax incentives.

The other practice enhancing dividend and capital prospects is the merger or acquisition route. Careers labeled as brilliant or genius have traversed this path. If a company acquires another that contributes $100 million to its earnings in the first year of its acquisition, assuming earnings before were unchanged, then it has shown "growth" of $100 million. The economy has not been a beneficiary of that spurious growth. Only the acquiring company can claim it. The market usually translates this acquisition positively. If it does it pays an appropriate reward. One of its most blatant and largest practitioners is regarded as the number one business genius. He certainly was when we count personal corporate plunder that he practiced with gusto comparable to his disguised no-growth acquisitions. This has come to be known as the adolescent theory of business success. Once he retired from the game, he discovered girls.

The growth by acquisition route has several advantages. It shows growth where none is. It can cover up decline by making it look like growth. It is a pregnant vehicle for staff reductions. We acquire these companies because they are poorly managed, so we pare them down immediately. This is another enhancement of the effects of the lower taxes on dividends and capital growth.

At the root of the power economics of deep staff reductions and growth by acquisition is the character of the men and women who pursue these policies. Our education system has been robbed of its value largely by replacing knowledge pursuit with training. The MBA degree is not uniquely the only symbol of training versus education, but it is certainly an important one. It is doubly important because as time has progressed, business decision makers are increasingly trained as MBAs. In earlier business history the leaders were men (and they were mostly men then) who came from diverse and substantive educational backgrounds. They had degrees in English literature, chemistry, political science, and similar fields of study that not only required thinking, but also taught it. Many had no degrees at all. They had a significantly broader understanding of the world and a thought horizon beyond the next five minutes. The current leadership crop is merely trained. The business barnyard is filled with one-trick ponies. It is somewhat more than symbolic that the source of the growth-discouraging tax reductions is the first MBA to occupy the presidency.

The MBA programs are not very subtle about their slim substance, either. New courses are invented year to year to accommodate fashion, and then they disappear as fashion does. Has anyone ever seen an advertisement promising a fast-track, part-time graduate degree for French civilization or international diplomacy? MBA program ads abound in them.

My favorite personal observation that may characterize the field was when I was observing a colleague busily reproducing many pages of text at our nonacademic workplace. We both taught at the university in the evenings. I asked out of mild curiosity what he was doing. He said that he was copying a set of notes he had gotten from someone else for an evening MBA course he was going to give. This was being done with his other-than-academic employer's paper and equipment, and on his employer's time. The course he was to teach was business ethics.

That subject had a brief spotlight some time ago when it was suspected that not many MBA students knew what it was. It has since faded from interest. Or do they now have one called corporate governance? If so, it needs some considerable polishing. There is nothing like a good euphemism. I suppose calling it something including the word "ethics" might imply there are some unethical things happening.

Aside from the pain inflicted by these business policies, there is a real question regarding the logic behind the tax breaks. Taxation policy is riddled with folklore that is taken as fact and has been for some time. There is, for example, absolutely no basis for the understanding that progressive taxes are inherently fair. In 1953, Blum and Kalven wrote an impressive essay in book form, *the uneasy case for progressive taxation*, which raised some legitimate doubts about the beliefs regarding progressive taxation. My point here is not to attempt to discredit the reasoning behind progressive taxation. Much of what we accept as fact about taxation and other social phenomena is not necessarily right. In fact, heresy as it may be in a world where nothing exists that is not data describable, I think that the common, if indemonstrable understanding about progressive taxation should be accepted. There is an intuitive rightness about it. Also we will never see a perfect tax system.

Even were the progressive personal income tax unquestionably fair in structure, it is so denatured of its progressivity that it cannot be judged as fair in that respect. Many tax avoidance methods are available and used. The corporate income tax is an even greater travesty in practice—its principle characteristic being that many high-earning corporations do not pay it.

Likewise, there is no real reason to expect that reducing taxes on dividends and capital gains will provide benefits other than the personal enrichment of stockholders. And it is my position that the effects are potentially harmful.

Consider first the nature of capital gains. Some of them derive from the merger and acquisition activities noted. They are not very effective in advancing the economy. They are accidental to the progress of the system. It is hard to envision enlightened self-interest as spreading benefits because of these activities. In some very important ways they increase concentration and monopoly power. Rarely does monopoly power benefit society. Why should there be special rewards for capital gains arising out of these situations? These circumstances are undoubtedly a major source of capital gains. I note that this statement is not in conflict with my previous observations about mergers and acquisitions and their not necessarily adding anything to the economy at large. They can enhance the stock valuations of the acquiring corporation. If a $1 billion company is acquired, it is likely to increase stock price by something on the order of the acquisition. Once more, why should the stockholders be rewarded by lower taxes as they sell their stock? This kind of economic activity is largely paper economics. There is nothing real produced in the economy thereby.

Lower taxation of dividends is equally founded on a slim base. The double taxation argument for lower dividend taxes is flawed also. Corporations have numerous avenues for tax avoidance. To call dividend taxes double taxes does not ring true. It is based more on the existence of a corporate income tax law than on the actual payment. Even if it was it paid regularly and fairly, it should be considered as a tax reflecting a return on the immense power that corporations have. But that, of course, is how they got the tax reductions they now enjoy. Yossarian, of Catch 22, continues to fly.

Lower dividend taxation is likewise ludicrous when we give an honest appraisal of how "smart" investors pick stocks that earn them high dividends or capital gains. There are logical explanations for many of their choices, but they have nothing to do with financial or economic sagacity. Insider information is one source. Surely the extent of this illegal activity is unknown, and just as certainly it is not a small part of knowledge in securities markets. It is no more limited to the cases that are discovered and prosecuted than is the extent of marital infidelity known to spouses who are being fooled.

Aside from illegal information sharing, there is also privileged information that is not available to all market participants. We have seen a lot of this amid the other scandals in the markets. Those who get and act on this information are not especially smart financially either. This is not to suggest that the actions and results from insider or privileged information always yield happy results to the investor. It does substantially improve the probability of success, though.

One of the glaring bedrocks of the continuum, the US Senate, gives substantial evidence of use of insider information. (*Journal of Quantitative Finance*, December 2004.) In a recent study demonstrating the financial genius of our US senators, they earned more than twice as much as the average investor per dollar invested. The authors of the study noted that our revered senators are cheating at a statistical 99 percent level of confidence. And we thought they were only political geniuses! If they could apply their system to reform of Social Security, no one would need to worry.

Finally, outside the aforementioned possibilities, securities investment is a gamble. A serious reading of recommendations or analyses and forecasting regarding securities tells anyone willing to think about what they have read that nothing is said. They are either ridiculously infused with pretended knowledge that is impossible for anyone to have or are so hedged that the stock purchaser may as well flip Bernoulli's famous coin. It is fundamentally pure chance. The buyer is either lucky or unlucky. Can we forget the magnificent high-powered economic analysis of Nobel Prize quality of First Capital? It dissolved rapidly and ignominiously because of a bit of bad luck in Belgium. Of all things!

So the reward of lower taxes is given to some who have access to information unavailable to others and to others who are lucky. These are not swashbuckling capitalists charging courageously forward and carrying the rest of us timid participants on their coattails. There is no logical reason to give additional rewards to this group through lower taxation.

As to the investment incentives that lower taxes are supposed to create, this is another of the unproven myths of our times. It is often demonstrated that our population, from the very poorest to the very richest, is generally so suffused with greed that really stupid chances are taken for very little money. Poor people throw money into slot machines with no returns. Many spend much money on lottery tickets with probabilities of winning in the mathematician's calculus of values approaching extremely close to zero. Wealthy people practice numerous instances of petty tax cheating for small amounts, and they are sometimes caught. She has certainly been picked on more than she need be, but remember the relatively small change that Martha Stewart gained. Aside from the notorious stock transactions, her trial brought out her normal attempts to charge personal expenses to her business that were sometimes rebuffed by her managers.

Many other examples of wealthy people acting with preposterous penurious greed are known. So these people are going to restrain their greed; that is, cut back on investment, if they have to pay 36 percent taxes rather than 15 percent. Not likely.

Aside from the MBA grip on business policy, there is a second educational pedigree that is similarly dominating. Attorneys, either in their roles as lobbyist influence peddlers or as occupants of seats in various legislatures, have a good grip on the government's piece of the moneypower continuum.

Lawyers are devoted to creating imaginary worlds. Their whole law school experience trains them to do this. The most successful ones are the most imaginative, as distinguished from creative. Follow any significant trial in the courts, and, objectively speaking, you have two groups of lawyers who are making up scenarios of fantasy. I suspect that many of them believe that this is the best way to get at the truth, but reasonable minds have excellent reason to doubt it. There are, of course, charlatan attorneys who have neither an interest in nor knowledge of the truth. These include some of our most famed.

Regardless of the ethical merits of the common practice of the law, it is a constructed world not necessarily closely related to reality. It is conceivable that many of our problems of the continuum relate to the strong influences of MBAs and lawyers. The first are trained in very narrow, mostly rote, methods of thinking. The second are trained to build unreal mental structures. Real thinking and creativity are not widespread among these groups.

It also is notable that no matter how rich the educational experiences of MBAs and lawyers may or may not be, there is still the problem of having people trained along narrow lines in complex organizations.

A similar criticism would apply in great part if there were other dominant educational specialties riding the moneypower continuum. Say people with degrees in philosophy and Russian history replaced the MBAs and lawyers. We might get some deeper thinking but would still have unnecessarily confined thought patterns. Corporations and Congresses need diversity of thinkers to be really good. This is lacking today, and its absence is not at all understood.

7

Overall Observations

P art of the divergences from purpose that I have been treating arises from clutter. Each of the noted institutions goes beyond its purposes. They become multipurpose, and, much like multipurpose tools, none of their functions are done as well as their single-purpose components were. In taking on additional activities, they lose their main ones and start overlapping. This environment of opportunities compounds the difficulties of government, church, university, and business. Business has one advantage over the others here too. As happens frequently, when a corporation discovers that its diversification has gotten out of hand, it sells the pieces that are not performing. The church, university, and government are not so easily adjusted. Government does divest itself of some functions occasionally but by no means does much to clean out its poorly performing units in any regular way.

A great contributor to the abuses of nonfinancial corporations has been the relatively recent authority of financial institutions to enter multiple fields of finance that were previously limited by regulation to specialized banks, brokers, and the like, the most notorious being securities underwriting and analyses and recommendations in the same hands. This is a clear conflict that has been created and enjoyed by many.

Churches have expanded their social services while detracting from their special sacred purposes. This is very trendy and is supposed to reflect their involvement with people. But these kinds of activities often take over the institutions, and they forget what they are supposed to be about. Monastic life has often gone through reforms historically, as have religions in general. A reexamination of lay religious life is just as important.

The academy is nearly totally engaged in training, forgetting the fundamentals of true education. It has also mistaken as educational enlargement a variety of activities requiring students to volunteer for numerous social causes. I wonder how many potentially useful adults in volunteer fields are soured by the blatant or subtle pressures to do good while they are in school. I don't wonder that these requirements contribute little to the purpose of real education and may be a hindrance.

How did things get this way? That is, how did the continuum infect all of our important institutions? Not much has really changed in essence among the institutions of today and their predecessors. It's rather that the reach and power of today is extraordinary. Tools and other resources are bigger and more easily available. The misinformed who aspire to great wealth without a clue as to how to get there, but who are convinced they will get there, also feed on the oceans of greed that engulf us.

We also confuse change with progress. Progress, in itself is a new idea in history. J. B. Bury's *The Idea of Progress*, the most respected statement on the subject, demonstrates that progress as an idea as we think of it today is a post-Renaissance idea. Its most famous original thinker about it is Francis Bacon. This means that it has been with us as a widespread idea for only two hundred to three hundred years.

Regarding the difference between progress and change alone, Evelyn Underhill observes that to grow is to change. That idea does not reverse itself. To change is not necessarily to grow.

As for the continuum and its broad dominance, there are always people in power positions, whether they are cardinals, provosts, or CEOs, who are clearly interested exclusively in self-service rather than institutional service. They can form a nucleus for the problems.

More significant is the humanity, which we all share, wherein we rarely perceive our own sins, much less feel contrition. True, public sinners, that is, those who get caught, will confess and maybe find Jesus or go into rehabilitation. If they are too poor for rehabilitation, they can fall back on their terrible childhood excuse. I felt sympathy for Governor Corzine, who could only say he was sorry for not wearing a seatbelt when he got banged up in an accident. There are no seat belt rehabilitation institutions. He did not claim a messed up childhood.

But the rest of us think we can do no wrong.

Institutions, being made up of humans, are likewise disposed. They can readily believe, as they see it, that despite some imperfections they are educating, spiritualizing, and employing. Their self-assessed flaws are insignificant. A current sly variation on this attitude, when they are caught in a public indiscretion, is their noble proclamation of their acceptance of responsibility. So, what then? So, nothing. Public relations have been satisfied.

Further along, a mentality develops in people with power that they are not accountable for their actions, as are ordinary people. They are above wrongdoing because they have attained so much. Often this does not have to be really so much attainment. (Some of them remind me of very young infants who take pride in their achievement when they sneeze. But they soon become more sophisticated in understanding that a sneeze arises from some cause other than their efforts.) This notion of lack of accountability is demonstrated frequently in public. I think it is an unassailable frame of mind as to its existence. It ranges from pedophile priests to a corporate criminal apparently unable to see that what he or she did was wrong.

Ultimately, embracing all of the levels of explanation of these problems is the construction of the quantum mind. According to Johnjoe McFadden in his book *Quantum Evolution*, our brains include a level of electromagnetic field that McFadden concludes is the basis of free will in us, and he suggests it is also the source of creative thought. I see free will and creative thought as completely intertwined in fact and specifically in the posited electromagnetic field. The field arises out of all the other electromagnetic activities of the brain generated in the neurons and their firing synapses. The latter are the multiple ordinary events of human activity. Most of them, such as our body motor motions, are not the subject of particular conscious thought. Unless we have an injured leg, we give little thought to walking. There are similar thought processes that engage practically no intellectual energies of note. These are probably most of what we think. Stop and think! This is something that we tell ourselves at times or that someone else does. It means that usually we don't.

The highest level of consciousness, the humanity defining place and process in us, is that electromagnetic field operating at the top of our brains. When we set this in play we are at our peak. We are creative in the service of morality or immorality. Conscious humans operate, ordinarily, at the level of consciousness below the consciousness electromagnetic field. The large and small flaws addressed herein regarding church, corporation, government, and university are resident in the brain activity about which little is delivered by way of careful thought. All is routine. Venial sins, whether corporate, academic, governmental, or clerical, eventually grow into routine mortal sins with nobody noticing, except for the victims. Even the victims often eventually acquiesce.

But institutional mortality does happen. Too much stupidity and venality do sometimes take their toll. Alternatively, saints, scholars, genuine entrepreneurs, and true leaders come forward, but probably not often enough. We must, despite the unfavorable odds, seek these people.

8

Putting Some of These Things Together

First, here's a quick review of microeconomics and market behavior. Students are taught that the base for market understanding is the model of perfect competition. It is described as a theoretical construct that is a basis for understanding how more realistic markets work. Its outstanding characteristic for our purposes is that no participant in this theoretical model has any power. Sales volume and prices are the result of pure market forces. In other words, it is an ideal that anyone striving for a sizable piece of the moneypower continuum would disdain completely. Not only is it a theoretical ideal, but it also is quite the opposite of any conception of business activity, as we understand it. There would be practically no place for a first-rate, self-respecting MBA in such a place. Strategies would be very simple, and earnings would be modest. That is to say, the continuum does not exist in that imaginary world. It is not there any more than it would be in a religion of pure spirituality aimed exclusively at aiding its communicants to increase their love of God, or in an academy totally dedicated to enlightenment, or in a government of the people, by the people, and especially for the people.

After the perfectly competitive market is explored, the intellectual path through the more realistic market types becomes very fuzzy. In advanced graduate work, the nature of the subject is embraced by game theory.

Game theory is a sophisticated analysis of strategies for one or more people or firms to achieve an objective that not all of them can reach. Outcomes may be very obvious, or they may be very vague (and realistically usually are.) The ideal is to be the winner in a zero sum game. This is another way of saying winner takes all. Most games are not zero sum, hence the uncertainties.

Game theory is also a means of conducting war games. This is a telling point. Moneypower corporations are not engaging in economic competition but in a kind of warfare. It is often quite vicious.

It seems to me that the highly fashionable role of game theory in economics is a simple confirmation that the moneypower continuum has arrived in the subject matter. While there are some who do not consider game theory as economics, so far, they are losing the fight until the next new thing in academic fashion arrives. There is also something to be noted here about education and how things like game theory affect it, to the discredit of education.

Mankind has always been interested in foreseeing the future. Divinations, omens, and signs have been a serious part of what we think we need to know, despite their usual failure to tell us in fact what it is we want to know. These oracular attempts are frequently wrong, and when they are "right" a coin toss would have been as likely correct. Even today newspapers and other sources print astrological forecasts. Many people, including a recent president of the United States, seriously consider these and other astrological messages.

Since the age of the Enlightenment, many others consider such superstitions as the nonsense that they are. Yet in some ways we have almost superstitiously enshrined truth as exclusively founded in quantitative information. We are inclined to believe anything that is wrapped in numbers. Numbers, graphs, and data piles have become the omens and signs that guide us, often regardless of their validity or even outright fabrication. One of the most notorious examples is those studies demonstrating the positive economic value of sports venues.

Governments interested in building stadiums hire a consulting firm that invariably shows clearly the net income increases from the venture.

Just as invariably they turn out to be severely losing propositions. The worst examples in this category of divination are cities that host the Olympics.

So, the economist-analyst is little more than the king's oracle or whatever name the royal sorcerer was called. He or she tells the king what he wants to hear.

More subtle influences on truth, as opposed to outright lies, are the way we deal with forecasting in perfectly legitimate ways. Economics and meteorology are instances that illustrate the point. They sometimes appear to have become more inaccurate as time advances along with knowledge. In the case of economics, the problem has been made worse by the changes in the basic institutions that economists study. Global economics, which was thought to be a well understood closed system, seems less so lately. Really bizarre consumer behavior, especially in the United States, is another notable element that is unaccountable.

Perhaps the same may be said for meteorology. Weather patterns have been changing faster than knowledge can account for them. Global warming is just one big piece of the problem, unless you lived in the George Bush White House. Different drummers paced that parade.

Underlying the noted difficulties in weather and economics is our way of educating our forecasters. In both cases, fascination with methodology overwhelms the diviners. It is much like religions that lose sight of their real purposes and get lost in ceremony and ritual. Methodological techniques are enhanced with technology of software and its hardware base. These easily make technique appear to be knowledge. The people involved and their audiences agree that this error is truth.

Watching weather reports on television can be dazzling. Computer graphics and their associated data are all part of the showmanship. Whether the presenter of this magic or the audience is so impressed, nobody seems to notice the next day when yesterday's forecast missed the mark. This error is often a substantial one. If the forecast of the previous day was correct, the "as we told you yesterday" is smugly given to us. Usually no note of the big miss is made unless something like two feet of snow arrived rather than the two inches forecast.

Economic forecasting is somewhat different. There are many forecasts and, so, many prognosticators. Papers like the *Wall Street Journal* often give a scorecard. It runs like this. Six of the economists indicated that they expect mortgage interest rates to rise; four say they will fall; two see no change. The information is turned into an election. In the example, rising mortgage interest rates wins. It's not a good idea to make decisions for, say, home purchases this way.

These examples indicate the serious problem concerning the misdirection of educational efforts. The emphasis on methods and their technological base has several effects. It crowds out time for learning facile communication in speech and writing. This reinforces the aura of mystery and pseudoknowledge that various practitioners of the forecasting arts convey. When they speak or write about what they are doing and concluding, their primitive speech abilities and their often nearly impossible writing are impressive. Many readers and listeners misunderstand their communication handicaps as expressive of the arcane nature of the work.

A second effect is the self-delusion of the practitioners that they are in command of their subject matter. They are not. They organize and manipulate data and information and do it so cleverly as to believe that it is substantive knowledge. Students of economics become wrapped into and enamored of things like econometrics and game theory. Little economics is involved in their formal educations. Their mentors deeply encourage their membership in the cult. There is a similar environment in physics. String theory rules the roost, and it's part of the game to do string theory. More than that, membership is a survival and success requirement. This economics course regimen leaves out economics. It also leaves out thinking. They acquire the skills of a sophisticated software program residing on the hard drive of their brains. This is not thinking.

There is probably another restraint on meteorology. Many students take television courses. They study meteorology to become television performers. That should be enough in itself to discourage knowledge and thinking. Television has well-deserved notoriety as being no place for thinking.

There is a curious contrast between economics and meteorology. Economists are among the leaders of academic cult life. The word *economics* originates in the Greek, meaning household management, a rather mundane root for the esoterica of economics today.

The word *meteorology*, on its face, looks to the heavens. Meteors are strange and dangerous things spewing fire across the heavens and sometimes crashing into the planet with sufficient force to eliminate whole species. We look to the heavens for signs, divinations, and cults built around this looking. But meteorologists today are smiling, friendly, jocular personalities who endear themselves to us every day. The only cultic aspect for them is when they get praise or blame for the weather. But they always take this with affable good grace.

Returning to my theme, considering the world where the corporation is the greatest power, a curious set of aspirations guides it that are borrowed from the church and partly explains why things are as they are.

Here I address again the continuum in its threading through all of our institutions, forming them and bringing them closer together in character. The practices of the church are the model in which markets and corporations work. It is the actuality of the markets and the economy.

First, let's look at the worst aspects of religion—the psychological problems that it causes. Sometimes this is, and has been, ugly and violent. The Inquisitions of Catholicism, the jihads of Muslimism, the witch hunts of the Puritans, and many other examples can be cited. Regardless of the horrors of religious terrorism, it is and was inspired by what its perpetrators saw as walking with God. That is hardly an excuse but is an explanation with parallels in the corporation. Death and destruction in warfare are part of the enhancement of corporate profits and power. Highways and automobiles, food chemistry, and pharmaceuticals can be similar venues for unhappy effects on human health and existence. I'll pursue other parallels as I go through my explanation of how we must understand the corporation.

Regarding the horrors of religion past and present, I would argue that these perversions are not religion at all but are some awful combination of politics, social policy, and economics wrapped in a religious cloak. This is why what is erroneously understood as religion's methods are so adaptable to the corporation.

Throughout history there have been institutions that dominate mankind's life. Religion is the original and is still a deep power. At first it was the only force worth reckoning. The Old Testament is "testament" to that fact, as are the sacred books of other faiths. There are still regions of the world embracing religion as life nearly exclusively for many millions of people. Some other regions established rival institutions in the form of the secular state, but even the most secular, the constitutionally secular states, are not free of the influence of religion in politics and government. Think of the Christian fundamentalists (Catholic and Protestant) in the United States. Would they not love to establish their rules as the law? And are they not a force in the politics of the land? There are undoubtedly other competitor religions that would gladly help us all to salvation with their control of the government.

Regardless, the state exists and is quite powerful in many places, whether controlled by lovers of God or by those who barely recognize his existence. Instead of tithing, we pay taxes, often a multiple tithe.

The third force that has taken over great control of our lives is the corporation. It is the freshest and newest of the lot, and it is substantially subtler, because most of us think that God and the state are still in charge. Not so. The corporation has perfected the powers of its predecessors such as to excite envy and reluctant admiration. But what it has most effectively accomplished is to make the tools of religion into the sweetest of gatherers of moneypower. Neither state nor church is nearly as good any longer. So, while I have previously observed the business character of university and church and the moneypower essence of government, there is far more to it than that. The corporation has reached back into antiquity and become a supersecular, materialistic religion, despite its apparent antithesis to religion and the church. It is here where a good example of the continuum among the principal institutions, rather than their common internal moneypower continuum, comes into play. The dual continuums, the moneypower on its own and the strains of similarities among the institutions, support and enhance each other.

The first point of similarity between church and corporation flows from the indefinable character of the corporation. It changes continuously. The original mostly single-purpose nature of the institution and its predecessors, to spread risk for a single venture and then dissolve, has evolved into functions as wide as all creation. In relatively recent history the corporation, though possessed of its current formal structure, had strong constraints imposed. A corporation needed an act of the legislature in the state in which it was chartered. Its business purposes were quite specifically defined. It could not operate outside that definition.

Today there is no resemblance to the formalities of its beginnings as a permanent operation. It is legally defined and is subject to some limitations, but not much of constraints is pertinent. If we examine the things that corporations did a mere half century ago and compare them with today's, we can see how much change has occurred. These changes are more of the character of an organic evolution. The very loose charters permit substantial change to fit the environment. This character of the organization is a blessing and a curse. In this respect it strongly resembles religions. They adapt to what they see as their survival and prosperity needs. Those that don't, disappear.

Religion is mankind's search for God. It is bound by nonrational and irrational methods. God is not found in discursive reasoning, though deep thought is an aid on the path. The nonrational is pure prayer. The irrational is the superstitions inevitably barnacled to religious practice. The corporation has taken on these irrational characteristics and enlarged them well beyond the ambitions of any religion.

In practice this became apparent after World War II. The consumer became an object of manipulation and was successfully manipulated. Referring to the new circumstances, Satterthwaite (51) observes:

"This opened a new chapter in the industrial revolution. Where religion had once been the charge for the productive engine of capitalism, now consumption, driven by these new behavioral manipulative techniques, kept the engine of capitalism running at full steam."

We witness an incredible melding of the perceived welfare of humanity and the new very religious-like corporation. It is all materialistically based. The match between the desires of humanity and the ability of the corporation to provide them is akin to the deepest spirituality achievable with religion. But those who achieve that religious state in true religions are likely a small percentage of seekers. In the corporation and consumer matching, very large numbers of those seekers meet their goals. No religion ever approached the widespread sweetness of juncture of corporation and consumer that the church and communicants are supposed to gain. It is a materially besotted Nirvana, a transfiguration, a satori. Unfortunately, it is also utterly useless for humanity. It has no sustaining worth.

With the irrational base for its profits, the corporation itself is an increasingly irrational institution. It is a premiere evidence of nonrationality. It has the like ineffable nature of any good religion.

It is a universal and indefinable thing. It collectively dominates the resources of the world, especially in the richest regions. There is nothing to compete with it. No church and no government can rise above it. It has displaced them both without their demise, only their relative shrinkage. Of course, both church and state depend deeply on the corporation. Religious and state leaders are usually quite close to the corporation leaders. They are a troika with no doubt who is the lead and controlling horse. The academy is the recruitment and training base. So not only in the essence of the continuously adapting corporation is its nonrationality evident, but also in its ability to camouflage its role relative to the other institutions, hence appearing as something else to the world.

As to its irrationalities or superstitions, they are many. Certainly they are as numerous as those that freight true religions. The more formal aspects of operations and functions are based on entirely inapplicable models of a business. They are "understood" not much differently from a shop or small manufacturing enterprise. The financial and economic press speaks and thinks about them this way. Students learn about them in this context. Corporate bureaucrats manage them in this way, too. All this is just a set of useful superstitions having nothing to do with what actually goes on. Why does it not collapse because of the gap between the superstitions and what is?

The operatives of the corporation are much like the good clergy in religions, the good civil servants in governments, and the good educators in schools. They are not privy to the levers in the hands of the controlling elite, similar to church, government, and academy. So they see life and live it according to the myths and not according to the large realities affected by those in control. Indeed, the power exercisers need the myths as a shield against discovery of the real ways in which goals of their organizations are achieved, that is, the goals serving their personal well-being.

We can also say that none of the corporation's predecessor institutions collapse despite similar arrangements of their affairs. In all three cases it is the colossal space of waste that they inhabit. Very much a part of the ascendance of the corporation has been its ability to operate with a much larger margin of waste compared with the other two, though surely neither church nor state can be labeled slackers in this regard. Church abandons true prayer with numerous ceremonials that have little to do with mankind's search for God. They go after their markets by popularizing and attempting to become as "relevant" as they can. Vatican II reforms of the liturgy of the Catholic Church are a good example. They largely stripped the Mass from its beauty and dignity but with little effect on bringing more people into the church to witness this entertainment/hootenanny.

This kind of reform usually advances them to greater distances from real religion. Government is notorious with expenditures that are exceedingly wasteful. Various subsidies that remain in place long after their real need has disappeared are a common example. Perks and massive opportunities in government for stealing by legislators are other examples. Remember the extraordinary investment acumen of our senators noted above. State and local legislators are equally adept at stealing but generally tend to be more ham-handed in scooping from the public purse.

The corporation gives many hiding places to bureaucracy. Its accounting systems are mysteries, as I mentioned above, that are not even understood well by those sincerely trying, and offer inestimable opportunities for wasteful chicanery. Many products are designed to achieve repeated needs as they fall apart. No consumer is unaware of this.

The imposition of economic externalities is extensive beyond calculation. Externalities are costs that are created by the corporation but not paid by it. The public pays them. In fairness, it must be said that positive externalities are also possible, but that is not relevant because the external costs are immense and often irreversible. No matter how large the benefits might be, placing them against the costs is not a logical accounting. Many of these create secondary waste of terrible proportions in the heavy fouling of land, water, and air. In short, waste obviously is the protective envelope of the corporation; again, church and state are similarly situated but are far back from the corporation.

The academy has, as a clear business, also learned to expand its wastefulness. Tremendous varieties of courses are offered, which require financial outlays well beyond what would be needed for a well-ordered and spare curriculum that offered opportunities for honing intellectual skills rather than distracting from them. They come and go as fashion indicates, just as any business offering products in markets does. Horror of horrors, some of the course offerings are inspired by television programs. This is really mind in deep territory, both as lodged in the students, who require the new goods, and the faculties, who respond. I wondered once about new course offerings in forensic science. Why should that be, I wondered as I saw the offerings announced on a bulletin board. Shortly thereafter I noted in some news report that there was a successful television program with forensics as its theme. Is that not pitiful? Deeply embedded in this mound of waste in the colleges are the huge bureaucracies that are its engines.

I have addressed above the sports establishments, in which are undoubtedly the largest and most onerous waste.

Education, particularly "higher education," is cited as an example of a positive externality, or a benefit to society that is not captured in its price. The higher our educational levels, the greater the benefit to society. I think that claim has lost much of it relevance as college students are merely processed through a degree of no merit except to misguided predecessors in college who think the degree is necessary. The benefits they confer on society are becoming less and less as they become more lightly clad in knowledge.

Two other religiously based critical elements of the corporation further illustrate its power similar to the church, but better. Proselytizing to gather communicants is crucial. The multiple-media total immersion in advertising in daily life has become so ingrained into the communicants' psyches that they barely notice it any more. And it grows and grows. It grows in volume in its traditional media, and newer ones are frequently created. It would not surprise me soon to see something like St. Mary's Coca-Cola Church or Beth Israel Bank of America. The clergy would assure us that these namings were part of God's plan, of course. If professional sports venues can be so named, why not houses of God? Are not various sports as powerful an object of worship as what we think of as worship of God? Corporate advertising is certainly far more powerful in gaining and retaining communicants than the church's methods on which it is based. Think only of the common foundation of fear for advertising. Do you want to smell? Are your teeth not white? Religion preceded these fears with similar questions. Are you headed for hell? Will you be the left behind while the elect are Raptured?

Not much insight into advertising techniques is needed to observe its irrationality. Indeed, careful, rational advertising copy is nearly universally to be avoided. Superstition and irrationality are at the heart of advertising. For many religion adherents, their understanding of faith goes no further than superstition and irrationality. The corporation customer must be fooled. He must be convinced that material trivialities in large amounts are necessities. Without them, there is no happiness. More recent trends in advertising invoke no subtlety in their appeals. They are clear and consistent in making statements and creating images entirely irrelevant to the product. Simple-minded exhibitions of sexuality and appalling attempts at humor wrapped in the non sequitur are common. The acceptance of the irrational and tawdry by the consumer in great measure is further evidence of the failure of education. The interplay of insipid education, preposterous consumerism, religious-like superstition, and proselytizing methods combine in the success and ascendancy of the corporation as the apogee of the moneypower continuum.

In our society there are two rights that never appear in any political document or in any institutional charter of any kind but are the most universally respected. First is the right to advertise anywhere, anytime, and in any way. The second is closely related to the first. Substitute "copulate" for "advertise" in the first stated right. The two cardinal rights are not unrelated.

Aside from the irrational format for advertising, there is an even larger envelope of irrationality. Nobody really seems to know how effective it is. This manifests another range of waste that very definitely protects the power of corporations. At an advertising conference reported in the *Wall Street Journal*, a really curious exposition of the flaws of advertising and the thinking of its practitioners was announced, though the characters in this entertainment did not realize it.

One of the premiere ad agencies made a presentation on the use of econometrics in assessing effectiveness of specific ad campaigns. It was greeted with disdain by many of the participants. A rebuttal against the use of econometric methods was applauded with gusto.

This suggests several conclusions. The practitioners do not want to have their effectiveness exposed. Church, state, and academy are similarly disposed. This is a wise attitude, it seems to me, because it is likely that many of their efforts would prove to be anything but useful, even to those who pay for them, regardless of the resource waste they generate.

More revealing was the justification for opposing econometric evaluation. It came down to the notion that econometric analysis cannot measure the "buzz." Ah, religion in corporation clothes again. The ineffable, the indefinable buzz, sounding much like the voices many pseudomystics think they hear. Advertising is the mystical component of corporate religion. How sweet. Mystics of real religion have always had difficulties justifying themselves. Some have been burned at the stake. Some have been condemned by Vatican courts. Corporate mysticism should not be subjected to a similar fate. It cannot be judged.

It is a pity that the opponents of econometrics in evaluating advertising do not realize the potential value to them. An econometric model in the right hands would be even better than the rich wisdom of securities analysts. Tweak a variable or two, bump a parameter a bit, and this, all wrapped in mathematics and arcane language, easily proves the unquestionable value of the ad campaign. This would take the "*buzz*" to really ethereal levels.

Advertisers do have a problem with television, undoubtedly related to supersaturation. The ads seem to float by the viewers with little impact because they are absorbed into tiny minds as part of the "story." This is a curious example of success being failure. The ads are so completely absorbed into the viewers that they have no effect. One would expect that this would be a good thing for the advertisers, but they do not understand that the brain's anesthetizing of television fare eliminates human reaction of the kind the advertisers seek. It suggests the speculation that maybe intelligent programming could solve the problem. Alas, it is too late for that. The idiot's delight that television has become in this century, combined with the depths to which our schools have sunk (another noncoincidental correlation), poses a dilemma beyond resolution.

So the new wave is to do product placement. The *New York Times* story of October 2, 2005, aptly titled "When the Ad Turns into the Story Line," says that during the 2004–05 television season more than one hundred thousand product placements appeared on the six broadcast networks, with a value of $1.88 billion. (Was an econometric model used to calculate that number?) An executive television producer predicted a quantum leap above that amount in the next two years. This practically closes the loop between mindless television and its mindless viewers. We must have unquestioned worshipful faith; never think. Do the money powers not understand that those placements will also be absorbed into tiny minds without effect also? Or do they believe that subliminal mumbo jumbo will be working? Even if it did work, there must first be a mind on which it must impress. More likely, whether it works is of no importance. It's only that they "earn" large fees for their nonsense. Don't mess around with econometrics here.

Will ingenuity in ads ever end? I think it was the first, but I saw a magazine ad telling us to look for the Chrysler 300 in a movie. Product placement is not enough. It too must be advertised.

The operatives of the corporation, akin to the lesser clergy, are another feature. While it is diminishing recently, loyalty and devotion are characteristic of the corporate clergy. The preposterous 24/7 attitudes give a sense of deep devotion as strong as the most dedicated clergy in conventional religious organizations. Enhanced by the current multiple ties of the individual to the institution, it surpasses that of the old religious clergy. Beeper, e-mail, and cell phones make life for the corporate clergy something that blends with the corporation in entirely unprecedented ways. Put these devices together and include the opportunity thereby granted to work at home as part of the mix, and there is much trouble. In Haynes Johnson's *The Best of Times,* he notes the reality of all the superefficiencies of the devices I have just cited really result in people working more hours than ever before. They never end their workdays and go home. Their work goes home with them. I suppose it gives some of them an artificial sense of importance. They never seem to know that their lives are a nasty sliver of what is possible.

Many seem to have a bizarre pleasure in this no-life existence. Here too the meld of what was once an individual to the corporate being makes for a perverse spirituality of a depth that was never imagined except in a few individuals in the former religions. These were the perfect—those who had become one with God. In the religion of the corporation, the individual becomes completely submerged into the corporation. Of course, these various devices tying the person to the corporation are quite useful in giving the appearance of deep involvement without the reality. Many sanctimonious souls are regarded as holy in their religious communities, too. So we have the interesting inversion of church, state, and academy becoming businesses and the business corporation becoming religion.

The overriding sign of the religious essence of the new commanding social structure is the way of myth. Religions are dominated by myths. They are totally dependent on myth as guidance or as their system of beliefs. Rational thinking is not the norm in most of our human endeavors. Outside of the useful and valuable religious myths, we run our lives on mythical foundations also. We think that having a college degree means being educated. Our brains are bathed for many hours in the awful and stupid myths of television. The corporation is our most powerful myth maker, and that is why it has become the power that it is. Its mythology can be dangerous to humanity.

The guiding myth is that it is a market phenomenon. This myth is enhanced by conservative politics. Conservatives worship at the shrine of markets despite their flimsy grounds for existence. They reach back to Adam Smith as patron saint of markets. They never cite Smith's observation that whenever two or more businessmen meet, you can be sure they are conspiring to raise prices. The moneypower continuum is its reality; markets are a fragile framework useful only as rationalization. What are believed to be markets are often power centers for accumulating money profits.

The contemporary place of finance, which is a creation of a fantasy world, is maybe the truly astounding corporate emergence. Tax laws encouraging investment for retirement have brought a host of innocent but often greedy investors to the securities markets. Investment houses have welcomed them effusively. Corporations must show results that please investors and generate obscene levels of money for their managers. Standards of actual performance are as low as they can get—until someone comes up with a new scam.

Finance and real performance are nearly totally divorced. This is a special but integral manifestation of the continuum that is really socially embracing. John Bogle's *The Battle for the Soul of Capitalism* is to my mind the contemporary economics counterpart to Kevin Phillips' *American Theocracy* in politics. They are both interesting for their insights and analyses but also because of the backgrounds of the two authors. Bogle is fearless in condemning the practices of the financial industry, where he spent his life as an accomplished participant. Phillips is a conservative Republican tearing up the mainstream of

Republicanism today. Neither can be remotely considered a liberal attacking the conservative financial or political establishments. But their books portray some of the nastiest aspects in economics and politics of our day.

The financial world is a vague phantom of the economy. The political world is a disgraceful debasement of religion. It transmutes God to mammon. It is politics at its most base as it debases religion. Whether we speak of the financial moneypower continuum or the political, the continuum is the theme every bit as much as the time/space continuum is our physical reality. We can do little to alter time/space. Moneypower should be deeply altered.

9

The New Moneypower Continuum

As life roared along during the 1990s, we were all supposed to believe that there was a "New Economy." When the new economy dissolved into the bad old economy, the genius creators of the new economy somehow lost their high IQs and did not seem even to be very smart at all. It is conceivable that a contribution to the so-called dot.com bubble was the sorry state of education. Here was a collection of geniuses that were not the typical products of the educated middle class. Some never went to college. Others may have been the first wave of the mal-educated that our colleges were then turning out, and now continue to turn out, to run our economy. Their disdain for convention, no matter how valuable it may be, was part of the package. If this was the way things were, we can look to more of this in the future. It will get worse.

Some of the survivors, however, deserve credit for their accomplishments. They molded the corporate moneypower continuum into incredible (or to use one of their favorite clichés—awesome) levels of control. Aided by the expansion of the world market, which they were certainly instrumental in generating, they fully transcend any international levers of influence that governments traditionally have. They are here also unbound by diplomatic conventions that their predecessor moneypower states had. Governments also have lost interest in diplomacy other than that based on real or imagined power. Who needs it, with God telling them what to do? Many politicians believe this or at least believe that they walk with God.

This frontline position of the corporation continuum arrived sequentially from church to state and from state to corporation. Obviously the church and state did not disappear. They merely declined.

We have our choice between two broad political philosophies—conservative and liberal. Until recently, the conservative reigned.

The obvious political and economic position of the conservatives is to reduce government operations in society and depend on markets for social problem solutions. The second Bush administration might be characterized as guided by this principle: that government is best that does not govern at all.

Conservatives speak of matters such as the mettle testing of competition, freedom of enterprise, initiative, and the heroics of individualism. These clothes of that emperor are completely nonexistent. It is a huge opening for the corporation to rule. While there may be some elements of conspiracy in these activities, it is not a grand conspiracy at all. It is mostly what is happening by reason of the many environmental confluences of the time. This does not mean that is good, just that it is.

The super moneypower continuum is only possible under the form of the corporation with its limitless economic reach and its elusive, frequently re-forming nature. It changes as necessary to strengthen the continuum for its own purposes. This does not mean that it is a monolith guaranteed to be successful on its own terms in every case. Here, too, there are winners and losers. There have likewise been winners and losers among religions and states.

The corporation is not ruled by many strictures so that it cannot get around. It is tantamount to near absolute monarchy but far more powerful than were the original absolute monarchs. It is not democratic. It has very few limitations on how and where it will operate. The government of Germany cannot govern in France—try as it did in the past. The corporation of General Electric can operate in Germany, France, and almost anywhere it chooses. Google is even more impressive, both because it is a new thing and because it is nearly pure ephemera.

There is something instructive in looking at the power of GE, compared with that of Google. It points distinctly to the really new age. Between GE and Google, there was Microsoft. I use the past tense because Microsoft is passé; despite big efforts to be on the path again, it is lost.

GE, Microsoft, Google. They practically embrace all of economic history since the Industrial Revolution. The gap time between GE and Microsoft is short but is relatively long compared with the time space between Microsoft and Google.

GE is pure hardware and has lots of power but is now the old person on the post-church/state piece of the continuum. Microsoft, barely an adolescent, arrested about there. It is a deeply talented child star that never made it to adult stardom.

Google is well at the front. In simple terms, GE makes hard-surfaced things. Microsoft makes soft-surfaced things; Google makes things that are not classifiable, and we don't know where they are going yet.

You may have a GE refrigerator humming in your kitchen, at least between its breakdowns. Your computer is spinning away with a Windows operating system, and Microsoft's evolution beyond GE involves even more breakdowns. But if you need to find out how to get to the new house that your cousin just bought, or if you want to get a look at the basic tenets of Buddhism, or if you need a recipe for muffins, you know where to look and who to ask. It is right at the heart of our lives, and we know not yet how deeply it will burrow therein.

Google is just beginning. Already it proposes to place the sum of human knowledge in print at the press of a mouse button. When I was a child we used to read about a push-button society of the future. I believe that we thought of it as something that would serve us about our houses and other in-place environments as some kind of mechanical servants. As I grew older I thought about all of the incredible conveniences available to us as the outcome of that early thinking but hardly at the push of a button. Now, the universe is there at the push of a button or soon will be. Undoubtedly the burden of pushing a button will also be relieved with progress. It already is in many cases, but most of us still struggle with a mouse button.

Google also offers an illustration of investor irrational behavior. Its initial public offering of stock was blessed with so much money that Google actually did not know what to do with it all. In the first year during which these funds were gathered, a substantial portion of earnings came from interest earned from money just sitting in the bank. The stock was sold at an indecent price-earnings ratio. That is, a payback of the investment would require many more years than the life expectancy of most of the purchasers. This is faith. It is blessed with all the irrationality or superstition of real religious communicants.

What is further demonstrated by the GE-Microsoft-Google string is the really powerful ability of the corporation to metamorphose into anything we wish it to be. None of these three could exist in any other form but the corporation. But even a casual examination of each of them individually shows the extreme differences among them. It is as though millions of years of evolution of some natural creature were compressed into about a century. This is why so many difficult problems are created along with so much of potential for humanity. And we had better get started on the work of capturing that potential for us.

There has never been anything quite like the contemporary corporation. Its power and scope is enlarging not only by the internal changes it pursues and the expanding world markets but also by the transportation and communication technologies that are all part of inseparable forces in the corporation. The moneypower continuum is at its peak in the corporation. It is becoming a world government with no accountability to the citizenry. This heart of the corporation is not clearly evident, because we still think of it as a business form. Either we don't realize what is happening, or we don't care.

That we may not care follows from the other end of the political spectrum, the liberal philosophy of political economy. It and other supporting attitudes outside its ken have changed humanity. In its own and different way it has dehumanized us just as has the conservative philosophy of political economy. A large part of the growing dominance of the corporation is from this joint failure of politics.

From the liberal side, we expect that our settings such as schools, workplaces, churches, and governments will take care of us. We are dependent; we have usually receded from any personal responsibility. We are "victims" of self-inflicted diseases and other problems in life.

Students think that their schools will educate them as they coast through a curriculum. Those who belong to churches often think membership in whatever sense is the simple ticket to salvation, not to mention health and wealth. This outlook predominates.

It would be desirable and should be expected that there would be some accommodation between the institution destroying conservatives and the individuality destroying liberals. It is the nature of politics to compromise, bargain, and work out arrangements between opposing views and aims. We can see the value of conservative efforts to minimize overexpanding institutions but being held in check by the liberal preference for protecting these institutions. Similarly, the liberal penchant would be restrained by conservative emphasis on individuality. Democratic processes in politics are supposed to work this way.

In the politics of our time, it does not. The aim is always zero sum. Anything less is considered defeat. There is really no politics, only power. A view of the acrimony, rudeness, and ugly behavior of members of Congress is a simple indicator of my meaning here. When a vice president in a public statement tells a senator to go fuck himself, you get a bit of the flavor of congressional politics. This vice president also had a criminal chief of staff who published a novel that is unmitigated trash measured from any angle. This kind of a stinking mind should be confined to operating a pornographic store, not influencing actions of worldwide import.

I read a comment by a reporter some time ago about how he discovered what politics used to be. He was too young to remember the Kennedy-Nixon debates. He got tapes of those debates for review. He was struck by the courtesy with which the debaters treated each other. He observed that they knew that one of them was going to become president and deserved that respect. Such an environment is unimaginable today. The tremendous scope and depth of the moneypower continuum has been the reason for this. Even the stated policies of the opposing views are not valid because of the pursuit of maximizing the continuum values. This is in control. Many days it's hard to tell a liberal from a conservative.

10

How Does It Happen?

I think the forces that ride the continuum at the top of the corporations, churches, universities, and governments are likely necessary. In these and other institutions, they have always been there throughout human history. Often they have been discovered only in hindsight. In fact, in recent years a whole industry of sorts has developed that is devoted to proving that nobody who ever lived and had been given credit for achieving was any good. That includes Jesus and Moses. In the case of the latter, it was not so much that he was a bad guy; it's rather that he did not exist.

Books of this genre are often lucrative enterprises for their authors. I do not include, of course, balanced scholarly studies that show that some of our heroes were humans and were not the gods we manufactured. The trash book genre appeals to those who have been processed through our higher education system and thereby were convinced that they "have an education." They are a sufficiently large enough group to constitute a huge market for the product. It is similar to the large market of hysterical children who support our pantheon of musician artists.

But the CEOs, bishops, provosts, and the like who love the top and disdain the bottom, where the rest of us are placed, are probably similar to the bacteria inhabiting the human body that are necessary to its healthy functioning. Outside this special environment they may be poisonous, but inside the body or organization they are essential. In both biology and human institutions, they have a purpose. In both biology and our institutions they can become imbalanced and cause harm.

Maybe the reason we do not revolt against the moneypower continuum is because there are people involved who are sincerely trying to help achieve the ostensible goals of the organizations. I think they are being used as shields for the nefarious goals, but they do deserve credit and are a leavening influence. The good priests, rabbis, ministers of various stripes, and other religious, devoted laypersons in religious institutions are its soul. Honest business leaders do exist, as do honest academic and political administrators and politicians.

The two institutions wherein I have direct experience are maintained by their devoted and sincere workers. I marvel at the devotion of college faculty, who believe and work as though each student was truly interested in their subject matter, even though they know it is hardly the case. Most of them are not paid very well, either.

In government, I have also known hundreds of civil servants, both career and political appointees, who really believe that their mission is to achieve the legitimate goals of their organizations. Neither they nor the faculties are blithering naifs that do not understand what is really going on. They choose to ignore it so they may do what they can.

Finally, but obviously not incidentally, is the fact that there are good organizations from top to bottom. There are good women and men who run them for reasons other than immersion in the moneypower continuum. Even within the bad news organizations, there are still good people in command of some units. I may be wrong, but I think of Colin Powell here.

On a broader scale we still are blessed by wonders of powerful simplicity that give us humanity, as we all should be, but are not. In the midst of the religious wars of Christian and Muslim of the Crusades, there was Francis of Assisi. Even though he was involved in one crusade mission, this was an aberration from the rest of his life. In the nasty culture of our time, there was Rosa Parks. Rosa Parks is especially noteworthy in this age because she did a heroic thing and went about her life. She did not seek the celebrity of many others in her field of heroic endeavor. Many of those heroes are more agents of the moneypower continuum whose heroism is so well disguised as to be indiscernible. Even greater as regards our sweet powers are the many smaller-scale unknown Rosas and Francises—smaller scale and unknown, but infinitely more important to the world than anyone riding the crest of the continuum.

Despite the good things, we can see that the purposes of the moneypower continuum predominate.

Given the negative and positive observations on "How Does it Happen?" I conclude that there is a world homeostasis that keeps things going. It goes awry far too frequently. I think that it tends to bunch into periods when much is off balance and times when much is in balance. This is not to propose cyclicality as a base. Many of what we call cycles, other than natural ones, are more random than we recognize, but we need to attempt to find or impose order on our lives.

Nor should the suggested necessities mean bland acceptance. The hell of it is that we must fight and reform all of the time. The positive elements of our institutions must be bolstered, and the negative ones must be attacked. The further hell of it is that the games are always changing. That is the primary technique of the moneypower continuum. The rules apply to everyone but them.

They remind me of my beautiful young grandson. Play a board game with him, and you know exactly who will win. He changes the rules or makes up new ones as the game progresses. But he will learn as he matures.

It often appears that the problems of the kind I have addressed are ignored, and we just allow them to continue. This may be the case, as we observe government and corporate scandal so frequently and of such unbelievable extent that we wonder if anybody is in charge. There are some unsettling reasons why this may be the case. As time goes on, the depth of the continuum becomes greater. Resource bases become bigger. All of the institutions covered share in this expansion.

An added unpleasant aspect to the problem is that the required mechanism to reform is often the offending institutions themselves. Congress must reform itself. Corporate power is so great and is so linked with government that to break into that is extremely difficult. There must be either an extraordinary explosion of public disgust or some outside institutions manage to break in.

We see this more of late. State attorneys general wade successfully into problems that the federal government should have attacked. Federal agencies move in, smacking hard at the face of local and state corruption, because the locals ignore it. The citizens of Pennsylvania screamed so loud and long at the pure thievery of their legislators in giving themselves a huge illegal raise in salary that they rescinded it—just in time for the election.

11

The Emerging Order

For the various reasons that I have either noted or implied, what we call Western civilization is dominated or about to be dominated by the corporation as our controlling organization. This is particularly important because the rest of the world is doing its best to imitate Western civilization despite spirited denials in many places. The sharpest critics think that if they had our material goods, they would use them in a much more humane way or for the greater glory of God, whatever the name of God is. This is much like us within the sea of affluence who are not riotously wealthy but who are certain that if we were, we would use that wealth more sensibly or at least less scandalously than those who have it.

Regardless of whether the world wishes to be us in better ways, the dominance of the West is the world force. This does not ignore the big Eastern economies that are rapidly ascending. They have become what they are by adopting Western ways. The corporation is the vehicle of that force. This ultimately may be good or bad. It may merely be an update emergence, counterpart to when state replaced church as our key human institutional controller. There were bitter struggles. What was happening was not easily recognized.

Our contemporary problem may be that the corporation has powers akin to the early monarchies, which were largely abusive. It is at least curious that the heavy-duty corporations are, or were, based mostly in the society that led the world away from the monarchical abuses. The populating of the United States was accomplished by immigrants fleeing either royal or clerical oppression. We may need to consider the appropriate environment for the new-order corporation to serve us better, just as we did with the new-order state several centuries ago.

Should corporations become our institutional envelope replacing the state, we should not expect them to operate within some largely familiar format. In the context of its times, many of the ordinary lot of humanity never thought that the divine right of the king was a crock. So, whatever emerges from the corporation will be something new. Again, our world problem is that the corporation is nearly pure power; we do not know how to use it for humanity's betterment other than by the most vulgar materialism, and it is flawed even here.

Should the corporation be where I suggest that it may be, it is not noticeably apparent. We still have powerful religions and powerful states. Corporations have been around for some time. So where is the difference? The moneypower continuum explains this in historical as well as contemporary terms.

The institution that has the hardest grasp on the continuum holds the large hand. This is the corporation. Surely in terms of the money aspect of things this is clear. For the various reasons, it has emerged along the continuum line to unprecedented power as well. Similar historical paths have been trod by church and state successively.

Remember that it was not really so long ago that the prototype economy and polity for all of this in the United States was one where government was held well in check. The central government was a relatively small part of the economy and regarded itself as a minor player in the affairs of the people. It is now the most powerful government in the world and has inserted itself into the lives of its citizenry to an extent not conceivable by its founders. Its influence was not even hinted at today's level even seventy-five years ago. A powerful contributor to the world economy in terms of expenditures, its political power is also unchallenged, at least for the present. But the mantle is passing to the corporation, whether we perceive it or not. The corporation will advance in its influence as rapidly as did the state in our country but with the significantly larger backdrop of the world economy.

Positively thinking about a new order, we surely have little to be joyous about over the ways nation states have organized the world. Whether yet broadly recognized or not, the corporation as the emerged dominant institution of the world has a place beyond the academic and popular understanding of its role. However troubled and immersed in turmoil, there is little doubt that there is a world society of dimensions never before existing or possible. The reasons don't need another recitation. Historical instruments of managing or governing this society are as inappropriate as was the church to handling the societies when it lost out. Multinational quasi-governmental institutions are inadequate for several reasons.

Those in place do not really hold the power they would need. They are fragmented among regional bases and specializations such as the World Bank and the United Nations. Devising something rooted in regular notions of government will not work. The entity to be governed is entirely new. It is also a morass of contentiousness on political, religious, and economic ideas and practices.

Strangely, and this is I think is difficult to accept, in many ways the corporation is the vehicle that may well be the way to organize a world society eventually. It is well on the way, though carefully maintaining the myths of God and country. It has a perpetual life, and its flexibility is beyond any other institutions ever known.

Regarding those nominally in charge of world and regional management today, there is not much of a case to be made for their success. Any dispassionate look at the world today, and for some time into the past, shows not much for humanity to be proud of. Oh, there have been various golden ages of this or that; much human suffering often purchased them.

Of course, to look upon the corporation, per se, as the medium of salvation for us is ludicrous. Its extraordinary characteristics for good must be isolated, and its likewise extraordinary capacity for evil must be suppressed. This is not a task to be easily accomplished.

12

What Have These Strange Institutions Done to Us?

With the corporation's dominant place in the world and our lives, we should examine what this does to our behavior.

The corporation is a vehicle of greed. At this point it does not matter whether corporate greed is good or bad. Its rationalization of greed is profit maximization. That is a goal that is similar to religious scriptural passages, which have been studied and debated for centuries, and which remain difficult despite how much they have been worked over.

Profit maximizing has come in recent years to have something of a settled meaning. The difficult previous elements, such as whether it should be looking to long—or short-term profits, are not given much shrift today. Social questions such as the welfare of employees, which would affect profits, have shrunken to small concern. Neither the corporation nor government seems much disposed to care about the welfare of the citizens. Profit maximizing means achieving the highest value for the securities of the corporation, in whatever well—or ill-advised way. Its achievement is for the benefit, as usual, of those in control—not the owners, not society, but for those in control. This does not necessarily mean profit maximizing in the old sense, however confused the old idea could be. It can also be detrimental to profits and the organization. It has quite clearly been so in many recent notorious and not so notorious instances. Some poor fellows have even gone to jail because of this pursuit. It is the overriding goal of the corporation, regardless of its merits. There is a kind of comfort in this, as we at least know what they are all about.

Profit maximizing, in its present form of enriching those in control rather than the stockholders, is a bad new kind of greed because it is a distorting activity. As the corporation is our premiere organization, it affects us in ways other than those addressed in the chapter on it. We may begin with a look at greed outside it but generated by it at least partly. It must be admitted that humanity has always been capable of greed, quite apart from and prior to the corporation. What makes things somewhat different today is that we see the great success of the corporation; we are educated in greed, and that education centers on the corporation and uses its methods.

Greed is irrational. Greedy pursuit is unnatural behavior that clouds or eliminates some of the most important things in our lives. It reduces our maturity and attention to other matters in our lives. It consumes.

Bogle frequently refers to greed in just about every aspect of the network of the financial community.

"Surely greed, naiveté, and the absence of common sense plagued too many stock buyers, and aggressive sellers capitalized on the popular delusions and madness of the investing crowds."

"Herbert Hoover said, 'You know, the only trouble with capitalism is capitalists. They're too darn greedy'" (24). This statement was made during a time that one of his party successors would have called a kinder, gentler time.

Greed is not limited to the pursuit of money. We have expanded its scope and tied it to many other of our life pursuits. We are clearly greedy for sex, food, and endless material possessions. We pay our prices for those things. Sexually transmitted diseases, a variety of health problems associated with overeating, and too much drinking afflict too many of us. We have merely absorbed these problems into our culture, for the most part, and we rarely recognize them anymore. This is just the way things are. Each generation assumes that what at one time were rightfully considered as horrors, are simply part of the game of life. And we also have the astounding capacity for adding to the list regularly. A bit of righteous indignation might help here. Often we regard those at the forefront of these activities as public heroes or heroines. Think of eating contests. Think of the hugeness of football players—the role models for youth—and chronological adults, if not psychological adults, in sports, entertainment, and many other treasured pieces of our world.

Our plentiful possessions are often worthless toys. Mental health problems are apparently experienced on an ever-expanding scale. If some form of nasty behavior becomes too widespread, we call it a disease, or at least a syndrome. We have developed a grand array to excuse almost anything.

We are so besotted with the many forms of greed that we have become a society of mean children. We treat each other with rudeness and disrespect. We seem willing to use any means to gain our greedy goals. We have few limits on behavior. We have tacitly and directly defined allowable human behavior as about anything that we wish to do. There is no distinction between private and public behavior.

In a *Wall Street Journal* article of January 17, 2006, reporter Loretta Chao addresses our rudeness. Not only does our rudeness cost us psychologically, but also there is evidence of its economic effects in the workplace.

I don't think I ever heard or read about anything as inhumanly rude as an incident concerning someone I know whose father was killed in a coal mine accident. The company reported the horrible news by telephone to his wife. Ugly and heartless as that was, the story gets worse. His wife was not at home when the call came, so they left a message telling of her husband's death.

Part of the difficulty of dealing with all of these problems we have created in our lives is that, looking at them individually, we can often justifiably say they are not so bad. Their sum is what gives us the character of a society of nasty children.

Let's trace a few of them. We begin with something holy. Going to a Catholic Mass on a summer Sunday morning is a revolting experience. A good many attendees are dressed for a kind of slobs' picnic. Many of those bodies haphazardly clad give ample evidence, incidentally, of our greed for food. If we cannot even pay deference to God, is there hope for decorum as regards dress? No, there is no hope; real observation attests to this. Church, workplace, restaurant, classroom, anyplace, is just another location to display our disdain and indifference. We are free spirits. We are educated people that rise above convention.

The antisuit, jeans culture is a great illustration, or was. (Suits seem to be making a comeback. Even the NBA has decided that its players should wear them off court on public occasions. This is a little strange because their playing uniforms have long been designed in the spirit of the lines of Groucho Marx's suits.) To wear a suit is considered a mark of real inferiority—slavery to convention, a weak thinker. Jeans are a display of the antithesis of all these things. They just don't get that their pitiful display is a substantially greater immersion in convention than a suit ever was. Suit wearers did not wear them for everything. Jeans wearers do.

Is casual dress, in itself, a wicked thing? No, of course not. It is merely one reflection of how little we value ourselves. Dress, especially in a high-income society, is an indicator of standards that are valuable. It conveys respect for others and for ourselves. It helps to define the special or important character of different occasions. True, it has been overdone in the past and has been a source of mean class distinctions. But it doesn't have to be. The jeans culture is no more a leveler than were the different standards of dress in the past. Hundreds of dollars can be spent on a pair of jeans, obviously marking the wearer as superior to the "nobody" in ordinary jeans.

Many have found ways to compensate for the drab informality. The masochistic practices of body piercing and tattooing have two functions for their practitioners. They make up for the otherwise casual adorning of their bodies. They reinforce disdain for the rest of us and for themselves.

Partly following from this casual dress, that is, dress that was in the past only worn in the comfort of home, privacy in other dimensions has likewise been abandoned. Despite the great public stress placed on our right to privacy, we behave with total disregard for it. People go on television and reveal things to the world about themselves that should be a source of shame, if anybody remembers what that means. Millions shamelessly and pleasurably watch these exhibitions.

In John Ciardi's translation of *The Divine Comedy, The Inferno, and Canto XXX,* his introduction to the *Canto* explains how Dante is ashamed by his fascination with the abuse that Simon and Master Adam are inflicting on each other. Virgil tells Dante, "The wish to hear such baseness is degrading." Dante burns with shame.

> I was still standing, fixed upon these two when the master said to me: "Now keep on looking A little longer, and I quarrel with you."

> When I heard my master raise his voice to me, I wheeled about with such a start of shame that I grow pale yet at the memory.

Virgil and Dante might have had that conversation about much of television watching today.

We have developed powerful supplements to privacy invasion beyond television. The ugliness of the ubiquitous cell phone is a notable one. How many conversations do we unwillingly hear in a day that reveal the apparent complete banality of the speaker's life? Others shout to the world things that should only be whispered. Most pitiful of all are those who believe that their usually screamed conversation for our benefit is to display their importance. It's a perfect indicator of their minuscule roles in life.

I note here that these patterns are childish. Kids are exhibitionists; they say anything in front of anybody, and they adore making noise of all kinds. It is inconceivable that except in periods of warfare, there was ever a noisier time in history than the present.

Contemporary music, whether live or heard electronically (actually it is all heard electronically) is best enjoyed by its audiences at deafening decibel levels. Almost unrelenting noise is integral to this music. Surely the continual immersion in bone-rattling noise not only causes physical harm, but emotional as well. It could be understandable if it were a phase of life that the uninformed youth goes through, but there are generations now who never outgrow this devotion. It's not much of a surprise, but those holding college degrees continue their life of noise with as much vigor as the high school dropout. This is one of the many indicators of failed education. It has not failed because values have not been absorbed. The values of decency and grace are not offered. This, in itself, is one of the indicators of the thin veneer applied by education versus anything real about it.

Aside from the most unpleasant aspects of noise-music, there are few public places where you can escape music, and most of it is awful. Restaurants, supermarkets, or mall stores, nowhere can you pursue the simple business for which the establishment is intended without music. Add to that the wanderers in stores who are being guided by cell phones, and getting out of the store as quickly as possible is a likely objective. In a world where shopping is such a widespread occupation and is practiced so fervently, I always wonder about the cell phone people. They seem incapable of the primitive job of buying things. Many of them now move about the store being guided by a force coming through the phone that directs them what to do. You wonder if they are not products of the MIT robotics lab. We have no selves, only personas.

Children are also usually fond of drawing attention to themselves. Look at me! So we define our aesthetic lives by the look-at-me rubric. We also have a decided preference for the fake. Almost any area of our lives is covered by the greed and look at me outlook, resulting in seizure of any excess available. Style and taste are so defined.

Ada Huxtable, the architectural critic, speaks to the strangeness of our constructed world in *The Unreal America: Architecture and Illusion*. She goes well beyond my notes below on housing and gardens. Theme parks, planned communities, and shopping centers are all spun out of imaginary stuff rooted in bad taste. She portrays our preference for the fake over the real very forcefully. Once again, it is the escape from the real by nasty children that we have become.

The appropriate symbol and artifact of our time most recently is the Hummer, the civilian model of the war machine. That is bad enough. I think it is the otherwise ugliest car ever to run on the road and maybe the ugliest legal product of any kind. This appalling machine goes beyond its surface repulsion. It speaks to brutality and dominance. A columnist recently wrote about a sticker he saw on an SUV that read, "I want to kill you." The Hummer doesn't need the sign. It says it without words. I cannot imagine what a pot of festering insecurities motivates anyone to buy that vehicle as a private car.

I pass a house occasionally that is a site that sums much of the look-at-me greed spectrum. It is a McMansion surrounded by grotesque landscaping, with a Hummer in the driveway. The house must have been designed with a commission to make it as ugly and expensive as possible. The architect executed that commission perfectly. The Hummer is a perfect complement. The landscaping pulls it all together.

Life's core necessities (food, housing, clothing, and transportation) in our prosperity have been converted to symbols having little to do with their purposes. Or their purposes have changed to altogether different things.

Housing, usually the largest single expenditure for most families, is now viewed as an investment. The expected continual appreciation in value, a questionable game for most, bolsters this attitude. It was in the 1990s and early 2000s, a pointless exercise as houses are sold, and sellers buy up and usually increase their indebtedness. The net gain over periods of time is close to zero. In the midst of this phenomenon, along with other attitudes and customs, the house has no relationship to individuals and families. It is merely an investment, another source of affluent excessive display. (Since this was first written, the price has been paid with the complete collapse of the housing market. It will take many years for recovery.)

In terms of numbers of rooms and their sizes, the house is extraordinarily in excess of needs. It becomes more so considered in light of actual usage.

Both parents work, children are packed off to some institution as soon as possible, which is very early in their lives, well under age one, and the house is vacant for long periods of time. Granted, these arrangements are sometimes the result of dire economic necessity. For the most part, motivations for these arrangements are inspired by no real economic necessity.

Even weekends are times of vacancy. Parents run their children out and about doing quality time. (I await the genius that will convince enlightened parents to register their kids in a course in boredom. It will do wonders for the kids' psyches as an escape from frenetic activity that is their usual lot.)

Its owners do not care for the house. They do not clean it or cut its grass, and scant real cooking happens. It is a big box used for sleeping and watching television and not much more.

The automobile long preceded the house as a widespread device for display, but I wonder about it today. Except for the crazy children who regularly kill themselves drag racing on city streets or slamming at high speeds without seat belts into roadside trees, is the notion of pleasure driving of any relevance today? If so, where does it happen? I cannot imagine that sitting in the ugly traffic of our daily experience is any better in a $50,000 (or much more expensive) car than in an $18,000 one.

I have always enjoyed gardening. There is room for a little creativity, for making things more beautiful, and for modest exercise. I used to be amused when I'd pass a new home that obviously had a landscape contractor put in all the plants. The operating principle was clearly to maximize profits by squeezing into the site as many plants as possible. All the benefits of gardening are lost to the homeowner, but they are probably not interested in gardening. More recently there is a dismaying practice not only to do what is described, but also to aim at the grotesque. Strange topiaries and unusual plants dominate. Every plant is a showpiece, and collectively they become an unattractive blob. Gardens are often ugly. The simplicity of ordinary plants diversified by heights, colors, and textures that make a garden truly interesting and beautiful is replaced by an entirely opposite unaesthetic.

Granted there may be amateur gardens that are unattractive or sloppy, but at least they show evidence of some human touches. The professionals are simply grotesque. Weird shapes and color mixes in expensive abundance rule the professional domestic garden. They should not even be called gardens. They are just bad outdoor decorating. They do present a message of value from their owner's view. Consistently, with our corporation dictated values, the message clearly says, "Look at all the money I spent here."

Beyond these larger instruments of the look-at-me society, we see numerous smaller designations every day. I have a strong personal preference for not advertising much about myself in many of the petty ways that are common. I wonder about why so many people think it attaches importance to them. At the least, the practices are so widespread that we are all submerged within them, so few are actually distinguished by them.

Some of them go through transitions. Bumper stickers gave way to car window signs that have given way to magnetic ribbons.

Bumper stickers are now resurging along with magnetic ribbons, so proclamations of our worth are done in multimedia. I believe that the sum of the multiple proclamations festooning some vehicles is all the thoughts that their drivers possess, except for television and sports-inspired minimal brain functions akin to thinking.

What do we learn about the symbols that we love, and are they hiding something about us? Consider flying the flag. I live in a community that revels in the practice. The flags are really saying, "Look at what a great American I am!" Do we really need to know that? Now that we know it, of what use is that information to us? Has the flag waver been under suspicion of disloyalty? If so, the flag waving probably will not dispel the suspicion.

A very nice piece of loving parenting is the bumper sticker that proudly announces that the driver's kid is an honor student at (fill in the blank) School. I see so many of them in my area for a particular school that it must be a middle school version of the institute for advanced studies. Clearly the parent has transmitted genes of great intelligence, and the sticker tells of the wonderful person who has generated the brilliant child. You feel sorry for the kids whose parents' cars sit in the driveway with nude bumpers, though, as noted, there are probably only a few dim-witted kids propagated by inferior stock.

The counter to the honors stickers speaks so nicely to the American spirit: "My kid beat up your honor student." The first time I saw that one; I was stopped at a traffic light reading it from the bumper in front of me. I really laughed out loud. But then I noticed some implications that rang true. The sticker was on a beat up, old pickup truck, or as they are called in redneck territory (not a pejorative term to me) where I saw it, a pickup. The bed of the truck was littered with pieces of rusted, indefinable mechanical components that had probably been there for years. The driver sat under a long mane of greasy hair that implied that it was in conformity to a sect that forbids hair washing. You really had to feel sorry for his warrior child if indeed nurture trumps nature.

Magnetic ribbons apparently are available for dealing with any philosophical bent, social preference, political or religious belief, and much else. Two very popular ones are the yellow showing support for our troops and the pink for showing opposition to breast cancer. Again, is the former a sign of another great American? As to the latter, are there any people who are in favor of breast cancer?

Various symbols, signs, and activities surrounding hopes for cures for diseases imply some things about our attitudes. The fact that we have publicly politicized disease is something fairly new in humanity's approach to medicine. It implies and actually indicates that there are priorities for cures and that these are a matter of bargaining, with winners and losers. This just doesn't seem right to me.

I am confident that soon one of our many marketing geniuses will come up with ribbons expressing sets of the many obscenities, vulgarities, trash talk, and the rest that T-shirts now display. These thoughts cry for wider audiences. In 2006 a cheesesteak shop owner in Philadelphia attracted international attention by having a sign at his service counter saying that customers must order in English. It was somewhat amusing to see all the public officials making baseless threats that had no foundation in law, and they could do nothing, like it or not. At the time that this controversy was being aired in the media I walked through the shopping stretch in Philadelphia called The Gallery. A large woman was walking toward me with a T-shirt imprinted in three rows of sentiment that read: *Fuck You, Fuck You, Fuck You.* Nobody seemed to mind that. Look next for a magnetic ribbon similarly printed on a vehicle near you soon.

A favorite of mine is the college loyalty devices. I have never understood the intensity of loyalty to the state university of my residence, Pennsylvania. The fanaticism of its graduates goes on for the balance of their lives. They never get out of their sophomore year emotionally. They are perpetual undergraduates.

I read recently that there are paw prints that can be stuck on cars of Penn State loyalists. They are prints of the Nitanny Lion, though many are anatomically incorrect, despite Penn State's having a good school of agriculture that includes, I assume, courses in animal husbandry. I had seen many of them but had a completely wrong impression that puzzled me. The first set I saw was on a car that also had the elliptical frame of the dog food IAMS. I assumed, logically, that the two went together. The many times thereafter that I saw the paws I thought they signified loyalty to the dog food, not dear old State. I don't see the one interpretation as any stranger than the other.

The initials enclosed within an ellipse are a bit more mysterious. It is kind of a secret society. LBI, for example, is Long Beach Island in my area. Probably in some other place LBI might mean something else, a point that adds to the mystery of it all. But who is to know that but the initiates? The symbolical frame of the ellipse, the path of the planets' orbits is, I guess, a distant secret handshake equivalent. Most of the ones I see convey no information to me. I'd feel so left out but for the solace of their probably having no more cosmic significance than LBI.

I believe that the love of association with various formal and informal institutions is more than a meager attempt to reflect credit on their devotees. It is reaching for something outside ourselves that has little to do with a personal accomplishment. Does it not imply a lack of achievement that we try to fill in by giving an appearance of some importance? Usually also, the claims are related to a nostalgic past. But what are we doing in the present that merits attention? Maybe it's nothing.

The sum of all of these things is the loss of our individualism. I mean here genuine human individualism. The flamboyant individualism of business success believed about the past is gone also. Corporate bureaucracy has smothered much of that but has not created a better variety by any standard. The replacements are generally low-talent, small-energy minions. They are like a group of monks whose vow of obedience precludes thinking not permitted in the monastery. Theirs is certainly not a monastery devoted to God, of course.

We are further and further from being thinking individuals. Our brains are bathed in television that is the ugly, the stupid, and the often immoral. As also noted above, our greed is a perverting influence on much of our person, and finally there is that business of education.

We are now several generations of college graduates who are largely products of trade school training or hobby majors. Successions of lower and lower standards of performance make for deepening degeneration. We become less able to recognize the problem, as we are unable to generate individual thinking. A powerful override of this perversity is our mistaken belief that we are educated. This makes things considerably worse.

We are notoriously insensitive to preserving and enhancing natural resources. At least regarding natural resources there are organizations fighting our indifference. Education is unquestionably a significant factor in economic development. It is more influential than any other of our resources for growth. Yet little is being done to reverse the loss of this resource by making schools places of learning rather than playgrounds for the young at least up to their majority. Education is a renewable resource. It has degenerated to such levels that it will be almost as difficult to renew as the topsoil of so much of our land that we have destroyed.

Every one of these human follies, large and small, excepting education, when viewed in isolation from the rest could be seen as harmless. It is in taking them all together that we have created many of the problems that beset us.

It is not as though there is a modest amount of time spent or small numbers of people idly watching television. These are not small cliques of fans devoted to individual sports. It's not just a few freaky people who get tattooed or pierced, or buy obscene houses, or drive like fools, or any other of the points I have touched. Nor is it a few amusing bumper stickers or similar attempts at attention getting. These behaviors are pervasive. They are not universal but are very widespread. Our social and moral standards are so designed that given the many adherents to these practices, they are acceptable. Ain't we wonderful! Everything is okay.

The continuum and its effects that pervert most of the things we do, and the institutions in which we do them, leave us floating in a strange world. It is one where little is real. We are something less than the humans that we should be.

There are many popular indicators of these conditions, large and small. The trivial pervades not only in the depth of devotion to sports but in other forms of entertainment. Anime in film is another element in our perpetual childhood. It removes us to impossible worlds even more than other activities that save us from maturity. Splendid technology and, again, the sanctification of "art" give us the right to spend hours of enjoyment of cartoons. Doesn't "anime" add sophistication to cartoons? Let's not forget the comic books now called graphic novels either. It does not take much searching to find broad evidence of our mal-educated children, or of their nastiness.

Once cartoons were a short diversion among the selections presented along with the "feature presentation" at the movies. Now they are increasingly the feature presentation. Actors are proud being "the voice of . . ." Now, of course, movie audiences are supposed to be diverted by large-screen commercials blasted at them at deafening sound levels. They don't get enough of either noise or commercials from the multiple other sources of assault every day.

Actors who are the "voices of . . .," among others, are also proud to be paid for being in commercials of all kinds. I see Martin Scorsese in an American Express ad apparently agreeing that it is, "My card, my life." This is his life? This is genius? Is there no limit to the debasement to which we willingly stoop for money? It was not so long ago when Woody Allen had to sneak off to do Japanese commercials because it would have been unacceptable to be seen in a commercial message in the United States. Today, eminent actors such as James Earl Jones are seen not only as frequent commercial hucksters but assuming ludicrous postures of body and speech. This speaks, of course, again to the fact that the commercial and any associated real theatrical message are indistinguishable in the minds of audiences. Apparently this likewise applies to many of the artists of the theater.

Messages such as the cited "my card, my life" are a wonder in their own right. They abound in business. They have no meaning at all. If they did, Lord help us. But we do not want to tax the consumer brain with the burden of thinking.

We have maybe a dim understanding that our educational institutions are not reaching into us as they should. We devise things to make education better. "No child left behind" comes out to mean all children are left behind. They are not taught to learn but to pass tests. This is only a recent travesty. It has been built on many years of seriously weakened education. The Pew Institute did a study on the reading abilities of college students. The results were no surprise. In essence, they can't read very well. I was taken aback by seeing the authors of the study cite people who "graduated college." Maybe the funding was not sufficient, so they economized in the use of prepositions. What's the fuss about college students not being able to read? They don't see any good reason why they should.

Then we leave the increasingly long years of schooling to start our main events in life. We then often move into an equally strange place of career, but its strangeness is maybe not so bad because that is what the schooling prepared us for. We float further into unreality.

Next we get to the basics of establishing a personal social unit. We have made this into a sophisticated union well above convention because we are so well educated that we simply pair with another by living together. This union may or may not bring children, but it doesn't matter. If there are children, then they are little more than something we loosely possess. If things fall apart somehow, then we just go on to the next thing. The children, if there are any, often are appreciated only a bit more than the furniture that was jointly possessed. They are usually somewhat prepared for this because their relationship with what Dan Ackroyd, the comedian in the skit "Coneheads" on *Saturday Night Live*, called their "parental units" is distant anyhow.

Some do follow the path in a formal imitation of the institution of marriage as it has usually been known, but if things don't work, they move on also. Sometimes this generates such ugly public bitterness as to cause wonder how the marriage happened in the first place. Possibly the problems originate in the frequent marriage ceremonies that are just impossibly cute. The insipid quest for inept show biz settings for marriage ceremonies starts the whole thing out in debasement of what should be a serious and joyful occasion. It should not be a clown show. Right from the start it's just another fun time, so it need never be taken too seriously. And it isn't. Again, we dwell among schools, careers, and marriages that contribute nothing to our humanity. We live in an unpleasant fantasy.

One effect of all this, and it is a serious one, is the loss of humor. There is nothing more serious than good comedy. A few hours of reading reviews of television comedy programs confirms this without doubt. Television humor attempts are too pitiful to mean anything. They reflect well our minimal education and the other dimensions of our not real lives.

In recent years, I began to wonder why it became difficult to impossible to get a reaction to humor or sarcasm from my students. It was not always so. They are not so seriously immersed in their studies so as not to react to humor. I thought that because of their purposeful isolation from anything going on of interest to a cultivated mind, that they had no context to "get" an associated humorous observation.

Then one Sunday we had a brilliant young priest deliver a wonderfully insightful homily. (This is a rarity in itself.) He presented the homily wrapped in wonderful comedy. I was laughing and learning with deep pleasure. It was, and he does it this way often, a perfect combination of religious insight and the really serious frame of comedy.

Shortly after this performance/teaching started, I realized that no one else was laughing.

I recalled having a high school freshman course in music and art appreciation. One day our teacher brought in an album of *The Pirates of Penzance*. As he played it we all sat silently listening, thinking that this was *opera serio*, I suppose. Our behavior upset our teacher. We did not get it. Our teacher then was also a priest.

During the homily that elicited no response from the congregation, I thought that maybe they thought laughter was inappropriate, just as we did as students. But we were only thirteen years old. No, this considerably older congregation just no longer appreciated genuine humor. I was pleased to learn just at that moment that the problem about my students was not about them. It is the world at large. I was saddened to understand what a sorry bunch of humanity we have become. If we do not live in the midst of reality, then humor dies. Humor depends on incongruity. There is nothing funny now. There is nothing incongruous in our world. Or, it is all incongruous, which is not funny; it is pitiful.

The priest cited and a column by *New York Times* columnist Maureen Dowd offer some hope. I also hope there are still appreciative audiences somewhere. Ms. Dowd wrote a column on the death of her mother. Her mother lived into her nineties. It was beautiful tribute, and a hilarious piece of writing. I laughed aloud as I read it and cried simultaneously for her loss. I have a simple standard for theater criticism. If I laugh often, it is good. If I cry often, it is good. If I laugh in many places and cry in many others, it is great theater. Superb theater for me is if, during the performance, I laugh and cry simultaneously and frequently. As the British would say about Ms. Dowd's column, "Good show!"

We are almost entirely without standards of proper behavior. Rudeness and meanness are everyday encounters. Many perversities are now seen as virtues. There is no privacy, and we are surrounded by noise. There is nothing funny in those respects, either.

Every day we see a microcosm of what we are as a society. One wonders if many of the people who drive cars, or any vehicles, on our roads have a minimum of education. Often they seem not to be possessed of even the instinct for self-preservation. Daily news stories attest to this. Courtesy, playing by the rules, goes away when many turn the ignition key. Even when they are driving away from the church parking lot, it seems that God is surely not their copilot.

A recent heroine of our time summed up in an interview a good bit of what goes on. She put in a highly respectable performance in one of our premiere car races. In an interview printed in one of our leading news magazines, she spoke with some pride of her achievements in reckless and irresponsible speeding on the highways and the numerous speeding tickets she has gotten. As to her expectations of a goal on the racetrack, she said that if she got it, she would, "pee in my pants." Quite the little lady there. Quite the little newsmagazine that printed this story also. I hope she reaches her racing goal. I hope her pit crew stocks Depends in their toolboxes.

Her comment was a bit more tony than the one I heard walking along one day. It came from another young woman in conversation with a young man. She was well groomed and dressed, which is a sight not seen often. It seemed she had to have a medical procedure of some kind. She said to her gentleman companion that, every time she thinks of it, "I shit in my pants." I moved rapidly past them for fear she would think of it.

I have cited several instances of female vulgarity here. I am not picking on females as a sexist exercise. They are merely trying to match their male counterparts in rudeness and vulgarity and are doing quite well.

Probably the most pervasive activity incorporating all of the problems of the moneypower continuum and its nasty children is sports. Sports are essentially children's games. They are also powerful corporations saturated in greed. Their formats are brutally nasty behavior. Many of their participants engage in notorious to criminal behavior outside the playing field or arena. They occupy endless hours of time by millions of observers.

In many ways, they reflect what we have become.

13

The Many Economies

One outcome of all these strange institutions and human behaviors is the confusion of what happened in the economy for the decade straddling the end of the twentieth century and the beginning of the twenty-first. Interest rates were working in unusual ways. Housing sales kept moving up and up. The securities markets displayed patterns little understood. Consumer behavior charged ahead through obstacles that should block it. Fiscal policy was nonexistent, and monetary policy was an admitted puzzle to the chairman of the central bank. Incredible trade imbalances kept climbing. All sorts of bizarre events characterized the economy. All of these things came to their inevitable end in late 2007.

I read a statement by a PhD genius economist who runs a successful hedge fund. This says very nicely what it's all about. For some time his game was off. The fund was consistently losing. (Hedge funds are simple-minded gambling even more so than other forms of securities investing. They are wrapped in sophisticated mythology, including not only managers with PhDs in economics, but also some managed by Nobelists in economics. An infamous failure that took all the skills of the moneypower continuum to avoid collapse of the world monetary system was just such a fund managed by Nobelists.)

His fund's losses, he said, were caused by investors *who were behaving irrationally.* A homely version of that explanation is the maternal parade watcher commenting to her husband, "Everybody is out of step but our Johnny." His doctoral studies failed to inform him of probability theory that tells us, "Some days you lose, and some days you win."

To give him some credit, investors usually do act irrationally. He is just able sometimes to guess the paths of their irrational behavior, thinking it rational. When GM announces that it will get rid of thirty thousand employees and save $7 billion, the market jumps with glee. Investors never notice that the loss of thirty thousand jobs represents about $7 billion of purchasing power, regardless of a pointed observation by John Maynard Keynes of that simple fact eighty-some years ago. They never heard the anecdote about Walter Reuther being shown a new piece of equipment by a GM manager, proudly noting that it did the work of ten workers. Reuther asked how many cars that equipment would buy.

The descriptions of the hedge fund genius and the GM manager reinforce the idea that nobody seems to understand the economy anymore. I believe the problem is that there is no "the economy." We are a mix of unconnected economies that do not relate very well. Many of the reasons are because of the things that I have been describing so far. The ungluing of "the economy" is a result of the demise of markets. Market prices, as I noted above, are the information transmission system. The major components of the economy and the myriad of markets are tied by prices. Prices here mean the system of prices that float freely. They ebb and flow from the millions of decisions of buyers and sellers. They are a force unto themselves, where no one is specifically in control. This system is the core of economic freedom. It is closely aligned with political freedom too, and it has disappeared for the most part. Its replacement is the continuum. We have thereby lost much of our economic freedom and political freedom as well.

Let's take a group of activities in the system and consider them as separate economies, showing reasons why they can be so viewed. A recognizable collection would be consumer spending, investment spending, government expenditures, and net foreign spending—the familiar components of the gross domestic product. I will substitute financial markets for actual investment. There is, or historically was, a connection, and it's easier to illustrate my point with financial investment rather than with real investment. More to the point, financial markets have unquestionably floated into a universe well outside a strong relationship with real investment.

My thesis is that these are, of late, separate economies. The problem of not understanding what is happening in "the economy" is that there are multiple economies, not one. This can lead to the conclusion that management in any sense of the economy is not possible. Management objectives, if any, in one sector are not necessarily compatible with one or any of the others. And management of each sector is in different agents' hands. This is possible without the unifiers of a free market and price system.

We can dispense with the unimportant but noteworthy observation that the monetary values of any one of these economies is substantially larger than the economies of most nations in the world. Textbooks usually point out the number of corporation incomes that are larger than many economies' GDPs. I think our separate economies are a better comparison.

The noted weakening of real markets and price systems has translated GDP components into separate economies. Each component now flies on its own. The failures that are at the roots include increased nonrational behavior to a ghastly failure of politics. They flow from the moneypower continuum and its heavy greed. It is also a result of the myth that there are markets in an economic sense. Markets today are only an organizational entity, with little influence as markets per se. Their corresponding change with the evolution of the corporation has left markets as mere frameworks for the reality of the continuum. As corporations grow in the multiple dimensions that they have, markets shrink. That is, they shrink in their functioning as markets. As organizational devices they expand. They are just devices for the use of the corporation and its continuum. Much of this has been addressed at appropriate places in prior chapters. We have further examined their effects on our behavior. We now turn to their impact on the economy.

Consumer expenditures are by far the largest components of GDP or, as we now see them, the largest economy. It follows that any significant changes here would be important. From whenever the big bang origin of economics happened, consumer decisions have been assumed to be rational ones. Any textbook today will start with that assumption to explain the theory of demand.

For well over a decade, until recently, the economy of consumption expenditures has not flagged. It keeps growing. Numerous times the expectation that we cannot go on like this has not been realized. Nobody knows why this has been so, but it is clear that the behavior has not been rational. Billions of dollars of consumer debt have been accumulating. This has fed consumption of mounds of useless goods. Examples of people buying clothing that they never wear and ultimately donate to charity are not unusual. The debt to support these irrational expenditures is carried at exorbitant interest rates. Some of it has been financed with more reasonable home equity loans, but it is still debt. This is irrationally viewed as no problem because housing values will keep ascending. Even if this were so, it's only paper value. Is it rational to sell your house just to pay off a wonderful vacation, now only a pleasant memory? And, of course, housing values have now dropped off the cliff.

In the year 2004, the United States economy actually had a negative savings rate because the power of the consumption economy was so great. A negative savings rate is ordinarily a datum describing a very low-income economy. The previous experience of a negative savings rate for the United States was in 1933. We then were a really poor economy deeply into our most terrible depression. This negative savings rate is something of a triumph of consumerism. It doesn't get much better than that. It is evidence that the separate economy of consumer expenditures is untied completely from the other elements of the economy.

The poverty of our high-income economy of 2004 was real in economic terms because the rest of the world has done our saving for us. Huge amounts of debt are held by people and institutions around the world, especially China. This debt must be repaid at some time. It is unlikely that it will be done in an orderly, easy way. We don't know how it will happen, but it is inconceivable that it will not be a big problem for us.

The second dimension of the poverty represented by the negative savings rate in our high-income economy is more a matter of the spirit, but it is still understandable in economic terms. We have been so trained to appreciate only statistics over substance that we don't notice that our obscene level of consumption is not a good thing. The data are wonderful, but we are pigs who consume without purpose. I doubt that most of us with the means—whether by cash or debt—to consume at high levels ever think of asking if what we are about to purchase is something we need, or even if it is something that will afford lasting or even short-term pleasure. We are largely blind consumers.

Note here that the irrational consumer is supported by equally irrational business institutions. Banks that issue multiple credit cards to unreliable borrowers, or even reliable ones, are a good example. Institutional greed is their base, with no regard for the human misery they abet. Mortgage lenders support borrowers' indentured service beyond reason so that they may participate more fully in the look-at-me game. True, they are not their brother's keepers, but when the brother's keepers show up, if they do, the damage is great already. And, of course, the brother's keeper has shown up.

We could recast demand theory by dropping the rational consumer as its ground, but that would not help much. It would eliminate an unwarranted assumption but would not provide a replacement. Irrational behavior is difficult to analyze and more difficult to predict. In extreme cases, institutional confinement is the only solution. That's not much help here. A human counterpart to the theory of chaos in physics might be a clue as to what is needed intellectually to understand consumers. The history of economic theory is filled with attempts to use hard science models or analogies to explain economics. No outstanding examples of success can be offered.

Some contemporary writing on consumerism, such as I have suggested above, suggests clues to how we behave as consumers. Conclusions necessary to be drawn from these writings are not encouraging unless we want to accept a substantially redrawn characterization of our humanity. Irrationality in our behavior as purchasers of goods and services is general. At one time it appeared that the female was most characteristic of the shopper type. Today, that is no longer true.

Overall, it seems that consumer demand has little to do with the variables and determinants of demand in economics, except for one aspect—the catchall, "tastes." It is the tale that wags the consuming dog. When economists describe the determinants of demand, that is, those influences that, if they change will change the demand under scrutiny, three causes of change exist. The determinants are prices, incomes, and tastes. The usual emphatic influences have been prices (among substitute goods or complementary goods—a point of not much importance in the present context) and incomes. It is fair to say that these two are the elements in control as economics is taught and as is vaguely understood by many of us.

The category, "tastes" has usually been almost an afterthought. Or it captures, for purposes of intellectual tidiness, any change that is not explainable by prices or incomes. It is something more than flavors or styles. "Tastes" in this context means anything not attributable to the other two determinants. It is here that all of the tricks of the sellers are employed. The influence of the global, catchall category of tastes has become completely predominant in reality. This is not the way things are supposed to work, but they do. It also means that its nature is not given to economic analysis as ordinarily understood. In the world of consumer capitalism there are often no real economic factors but for far-out constraints. Some market prices do move demand in one or the other direction. If airline tickets become very expensive, fewer people fly, but there is a wide range of tolerable prices for airline tickets and many other consumer goods.

Markets are usually understood in terms of prices. Markets are taught to college undergraduates as based on prices. It is not so. There are few true markets. The most important "markets," as we call them, are administrative devices. Prices are determined by administrative decisions, not by market forces. There are price constraints on the decisions, but, as noted above, they are very flexible.

Returning to the matter of irrationality in markets, were we able to handle irrationality in some way, could it be consistent? Should really hard economic times descend upon the consumer economy, would we be forced to become rational? Very likely, but if irrationality is such a splendid force for prosperity, why not keep it in place? This is what the advertising industry does.

As to the independence of this first economy (consumption) from the others, think of monetary policy. Of what value would interest rate increases by the financial markets economy be when the consumer economy is regularly paying rates of 19 percent and more? During the period of the early 2000s when the Federal Reserve was continually attempting to raise interest rates, the only interest rate that increased was the Fed's target rate of the federal funds rate. Nothing else in that array of significant interest rates changed. And consumer spending continued to charge ahead. The inconsistent behavior of the data for consumers is testament to the free-floating consumer economy.

We should also note that there are much data and many measures of consumer behavior. Expenditures, consumer confidence, price indices, and many subcategories within them are part of the array. The reason for these measures is well founded on the quantitative importance of consumer expenditures in the GDP. More realistically, they are a reflection of the independent economy that is consumption. It has an irrational existence of its own that is only remotely connected to the other sectors of the economy or the GDP.

As Leach in *Land of Desire* demonstrates, we shifted at the end of World War II from production capitalism to consumer capitalism. Satherwaite in *Going Shopping* updates and reinforces this conclusion. The events of the early twenty-first century make it unquestionable. As I see it, we can observe that the consumer expenditures component of the GDP is a separate economy. In looking at our next "economy" we'll see another smashing series of behaviors that set it also apart as the second economy.

The second GDP piece is investment. Technically, it is real, private, domestic investment—machinery, equipment, and buildings put in place in the USA. There is not as much room for irrationality here, supposedly because these decisions are made by skilled thinkers. Surely mistakes will be made, but in the main the folly of constructing buildings or equipment thoughtlessly is not much in evidence. The only purpose of these undertakings is to increase sales of products to consumers, businesses, or governments. Irrational consumer spending does not infect business decisions except to increase expenditure for investment.

Two critical reasons account for the investment component to be understood as an independent economy. The connection to the monetary financing overlay to real investment and the way that economy functions is one. I will be addressing financial investment primarily. The second reason for considering investment as a separate economy is because of the methods of operation. The mainly monopoly power clearly sets investment apart. As this has been worked over extensively in the materials on the corporation, it will be touched lightly here.

Financial markets are the medium of real investment. Here the funds for building housing, buying computers, and like activities are gathered. The funding for actual investment is only a small portion of total financial investment. The greatest amount of transactions occur in the secondary markets. The New York Stock Exchange is a notable example of a secondary market. While primary financing is included in its transactions, by far, buying and selling the same old paper or data bits is its heart.

Who are these buyers and sellers, or financial investors? Well, there are amateurs and there are professionals. Sometimes the difference is difficult to discern. I noted some pages back that the professionals are really the people who have access to special information, legally or otherwise. The ranks of the amateurs are probably growing because of the necessity for almost everyone to provide for themselves after their working lives are over. Some of the amateurs deal directly with the market, others via mutual funds. In any event, the amateur winners are so mainly by luck. As John Bogle observes, mutual funds have added another substantial layer of fraud to the investment process. In many respects, mutual funds have been substantially perverted beyond their original purpose. They were started mainly to give the investor who did not wish to hazard selections of individual securities the protection of securities spread over a number of corporations and industries so that losses could be offset by gains in the mutual package. Today, as Bogle tells us, the array of specialized funds gathered into one overall fund management makes the choices little different from choosing individual stocks.

Again, rational behavior is not the hallmark of these arrangements. The mutuals are rational only in that they sweep large amounts of money into the bank accounts of their mangers. The system is not supposed to work that way. It was designed to benefit the investors. Those in control manipulate the continuum for themselves. The supposed beneficiaries come in last. This is to the detriment of the investors.

More irrationality in this investment economy shines through the ascribed causes of daily market fluctuations by what are usually trivial events. Oil is up two dollars; the market is down. Oil is down two dollars; the market is up. Or, the relationships may be reversed. IBM shows a profit; the market is up. We are all familiar with the daily ritual for the financial news. Sometimes, it is admitted that nobody really knows why the market on a particular day or for a particular time is behaving as it does. (Note here that I say that the market "behaves." This is the ordinary way of expression. It indicates partially my point that it is an independent beast or economy.) The admission of no understanding is not made nearly as often as it is the case. The financial press picks a few pieces of change and decides that these were the causes of happenings in the financial markets that day. More likely this is true all of the time unless some earth-rocking political event happens.

The problem posed by irrational financial investment behavior is that it can lead to substantial unearned benefits to a company or substantial unearned losses to another. If the herd is stampeded into believing that LOSER Inc. is a hot investment, many benefits accrue to the company and, of course, its managers. Resources are distorted in distribution initially. Then when LOSER Inc. performs to its real standard, resources are dissolved or seriously weakened. This irrationality is aided significantly by the analysts/promoters, among others.

At the opposite pole of financial investment irrationality, a well-managed firm in temporary difficulty that could be resolved with care and time is pummeled by the financial market. Recovery from this blow is extremely difficult. Often it can't be done. This can cause harm that is not necessary and that worsens the problem. Curable economic illnesses are not permitted. As politics is now a vicious zero sum game, so is business. This is to be expected, as markets and corporations are nearly pure politics anyway.

Granted, the winners and losers could be described as outcomes of market forces. But in the world of business we have allowed to arise, naming these forces as market results is akin to calling a tsunami a tidal flow.

The two components usually listed first in GDP, consumption and investment expenditures, show serious deviations from their myths, or their supposed base in rational human behavior. Granted, the professional investors that we have described do behave rationally, however illicitly. But their activities are not at all related to investment as an economic phenomenon. And it is the kind of rational behavior that in other human endeavors might lead to incarceration, as it occasionally does for its players in the financial markets, though not nearly as often as it should.

The financial investment activities have become a really separate economy. Real investment becomes secondary. With mutual funds controlling so many corporations and with managers of these funds paying huge sums to separate management firms and doing no management themselves, the nexus between these activities and "the economy" is entirely broken.

Just a few of the nuggets of wisdom presented by John C. Bogle in *The Battle for the Soul of Capitalism* make it clear that not only is investment a separate economy but that financial investment is entirely divorced from the requirements of real, long-term economic investment. This means certainly that the long-term prosperity for the economy is in serious jeopardy too. From Bogle (76):

"With its 52 percent ownership position in corporate America, the Institutional 100 is the King Kong of investment America."

The Institutional 100 is made up of the one hundred largest money managers, such as Fidelity Investments and Merrill Lynch.

Regarding my observations above on the wisdom of security analysts, Bogle (99) writes:

"A study of 500,000 earnings forecasts from 1974 to 1996 found that the odds that a security analyst could forecast, with the help of company guidance, to within 5% of the actual earnings reported by the corporation for ten consecutive quarters were one in 200,000."

My observation that the investment economy is a separate economy is bolstered by Bogle's thesis that capitalism has been transformed from owners' capitalism to managers' capitalism. This is an obvious parallel with that of capitalism's transformation from production capitalism to consumer capitalism. These two transformations have been fundamental to the breakup of "the economy" into the freewheeling components as separate economies.

Exacerbating the problems of investment is the domination of mutual funds noted just above and their change for the worse from stewards to hustlers. Ah, the sweetness of the continuum! Bogle (147) on the mutuals:

"Building a giant asset base is the easy way to produce higher fees and larger profits for the management company, who regularly collects its cut as a percentage of the asset pool. But higher fees come at the expense of the investors who own the funds."

And as he also explains, the management fees are paid regardless of how many millions the funds that they are supposedly managing lose.

Finally from Bogle (212), quoting Jack R. Mayer, former chief executive of Harvard Management Company:

"The investment business is a giant scam. Most people think they can find managers who can outperform, but most people are wrong. I will say that 85 percent to 90 percent of managers fail to match their benchmarks. Because managers have fees and incur transaction costs, you know that in aggregate they are deleting value."

Component number three, government expenditures, is a shambles from any perspective we might wish to examine it. Usually we think of "government" as the federal piece, but the GDP includes state and local government expenditures as well. These are uncontrollable as regards their impact on the economy. They simply happen. They are dictated by very close special interests, and in many states and many more local governments they are a pool for grand theft. Citizens are so accustomed to naked theft by local and state legislators and heads of governments, as well as staffs, that it is as though these bodies exist in Dante's Inferno, where many of their officials will undoubtedly reside some day. But it is the citizens who have abandoned all hope. No economic logic exists in state and local government. Their financial structures are large pools for patronage.

As to federal economic policies, until the election of President Obama they had disappeared. With conservative administrations, there is neither economic nor political policy. It is all business policy, however clothed. There is a logical case to be made here that business policy is economic policy, and it is. But it is not government economic policy. The latter has a wider scope than enrichment of the party faithful. Before the Obama administration, there were sixteen years during which fiscal policy evaporated. (President Clinton was in office during a period when there was little need for fiscal policy as an economic stabilizer.) Government taxes and expenditure are treated as business or household budgets. Despite that understanding, the budget had been managed as the worst kind of household or business management possible. Even on their own terms, governmental policies have been totally irrational. Taxes and expenditures are largely rewards for those connected to the political leadership. Stupidity, venality, and indifference to legitimate public need were the policy foundations. A remarkable new political philosophy emerged at many levels of government from local school boards to both ends of Pennsylvania Avenue and most of what is in between. This was the belief that the most outrageous government activities, from thievery to serving special interests exclusively, are readily achieved, with no one able or willing to do much about it. The horrors that have resulted should have been expected. They will continue to pile up.

Monetary policy has been the instrument of attempted stabilization for long stretches of recent times. It appears to have worked. But that was simply the result of right time, right place, as are most of the profundities of life. Prosperity for the most part and minimum slowdowns of the economy had allowed for monetary policy and its hero Alan Greenspan to take bows and many curtain calls of highly questionable merit. In more recent years, it has been impotent. It is merely the fiddle melody as the economy burns down.

The final GDP account is the net foreign investment account. So much of this activity is dictated by forces outside the domestic economy that it has always been a separate kind of economy. This is not so true when the various kinds of controls available, such as foreign exchange control, have been affected by government, but even then they usually end up damaged by various self-defeating elements. Merely as an aside here, at this writing our foreign account component of "the economy" has exhibited characteristics unprecedented in US economic history. None of them are regarded as blessings. It is thereby even more of a separate economy now. The massive trade deficits financed by unprecedented debt in the hands of foreigners are permitted to grow along with no apparent concern by our leaders. This huge foreign debt is also the base that permits us to consume more than we earn, as noted in the points on consumption expenditures.

Curiously, the international economy still retains elements of a market economy, but it is bolstered by moneypower continuum elements such as the refusal by leading national traders in agricultural goods to abandon subsidies. This results in holding poverty well in place in very poor countries. It is more than poverty. It is starvation.

The problem of the nonexistent economy is that there is no economy, but several separate ones wandering about on their own. We have no good way of dealing with this. The consumer economy is based largely on irrational behavior. Incessant and unrelenting advertising, to the point that most of us do not even know how we are being shamelessly and shamefully manipulated, encourages it. Aside from the manipulation, our excesses of consumption are so widespread, and not limited to an elite class, that they are unique in all of humanity's history. Unfortunately, the superexcesses of our current elites are beyond understanding but are seen as a model for our emulation. Investment has also spun off into a paper world equally as irrational as our consumption. At least for consumers there is some tangible possession, though we get practically no enjoyment from it. The paper world of investment often disappears completely for most of its game players. Government has become the money generator for its elected and appointed public servants (amusing term, that) and for its attached paragons of capitalist free market business leaders. For the present, our international accounts are unworkable. They reflect many of the problems above, so there is some connectedness among the economies in this respect. The problems of our international accounts will be solved. This is a certainty. They will be cured by brutal corrections, most likely by others not our leaders. Even if the political leadership should solve the problems, the pain will still be considerable. Serious neglect of a gangrenous leg will result in its amputation. In the case of the surgery for international economic problems, there won't even be anesthesia available.

Ultimately, the sum of the multiple problems as sketched herein comes down to the dissolution of important myths, which are not replaced by rational thinking because of the depths to which education has fallen in our society. Economics has become politics, and politics has become power struggles at all levels of our important institutions.

14

Solutions

It is no secret that untangling this mess will be extremely difficult. The only sure way is to convince God to enlighten all of us to pursue the good. We can safely disregard that prospect.

The solution is to attack the continuum, and there are some obvious, thus maybe impossible, ways to do this. Solutions depend on the goodwill and consequent actions of those reaping the benefits of the continuum. That is, we must enlist the foxes to guard the coops.

Election reforms are critical. The influence of money is such that if a candidate who is underfunded wins, it is seen as an extraordinary triumph of humanity. It is likely that the better-funded opposition committed an unpardonable gaff during the campaign. (All sins are pardonable, so gaffs are the killers.) Aside from big money always the winner, both candidates are running on money with politics something of an attachment.

There is no reason why almost all, if not all, elections should not be funded with public money. No private funding should ever be allowed. Rebuttals of this position usually say or imply that the system cannot function without the donations of vested interests. Maybe that would be an additional benefit, because the system functions poorly, once the mythology is stripped away. The public costs of election funding would undoubtedly be a minuscule portion of the tribute exacted from the present arrangements, which would be substantially reduced. We might have representatives in government who would govern, not devote themselves to the moneypower continuum.

The corporate wing of the continuum should be attacked by entirely new antitrust standards. The old standards were domestically based. They actually were the highest standards in the world at one time. Now they lag behind. The European Union's antitrust activities have been more emphatic. Mergers were approved in the United States that were shot down in Europe. The EEU dared to slam Microsoft, while it is permitted to play its old game as usual in the United States.

We should add performance to the standards of judgment as to whether companies could merge, for example, or whether they are adequately serving their markets. I don't mean here whether they are behaving as monopolists or not, but performance in general. Imagine what this would do to Microsoft. Just think of what the world would be were Microsoft the dominant automobile maker instead of software manufacturer. Every day most cars would just stop for a time. Some would inexplicably slow down as they rode along. Recalls would be entirely out of control. Consider some of our more notorious airlines. They should never be permitted to acquire any other businesses. Their records of service are an abomination. They seem to delight in torturing customers.

The scope for reform in financial markets is immense. There is no need to go over the many evils that are blatantly in need of correction. Reading John Bogle's list is enough, and he does not cover some things. The fact is that there is some prospect for achieving change here. Simply honestly pursuing the laws and regulations now in force would do much. Compared with electoral reform or educational reform, this one is relatively easy. Much success is reachable by having the will to do what is needed. The tools are there for much of the work.

The sins of organized religion are not so much of a concern. At least where membership is free to seek God in some other venue, the people do that. Many abandon religious life, at least formally. If the continuum becomes too much, to the jeopardy of real spiritual needs, viable options exist. This does not mean that criminal activities of churches should not be prosecuted. Too often they have been allowed to remain in the hands of the church, with little justice being served.

It would be a good, if an outrageous, idea to outlaw religious involvement in civic affairs. This means that religions should be free to minister to the souls of the faithful but leave civic matters to others. It was thought at one time in the history of the Western world that this had been achieved. It had not. Religion had merely wisely laid low. Its reassertion in the United States economy and politics is frightening. Surely politicians and voters should be expected to act in accord with their religious principles, such as they are, but they could never be allowed to cite them. Neither priest nor politician would be permitted to use overt religious principles or ruses to affect civic or political objectives. That alone would clean up politics as much as flushing the big money out of it. If truly religious people are concerned with the flavor of political events, they should fight with political and economic means, not on religious grounds. They can speak to God privately about these things through prayer, which is the only legitimate form of religious activity anyhow.

Obviously, there would be a problem of free speech here, but much of what is religiously inspired politicking is openly or strongly implicit hate speech. The abortionists hate the antiabortionists and vice versa. Much of it could be interpreted as religious bias. We would not tolerate comparable public racial bias in politics. Perhaps this would be a route to clarify minimizing religion in politics.

Ah, the academy. In many respects, this is the most difficult to reform. First, its myth power is intact and unshakeable. When people are hurt by their churches, governments, or corporations, they know it. They may be powerless to deal with the hurt, but they know that they are being wronged.

Educational damage is unrealized. Of course the innocent students subjected to violence in their schools realize what's going on. But this is another ugly problem. It is an unfortunate accident of education, no different from what we experience on our highways or the multiple settings for violence that we allow in the name of freedom.

"Get all the education you can, kid." So the kid goes after it but is never told what it is. The kid is processed through various mills, even to a PhD, LLB, (Bachelor of Laws) or any number of labels attesting to educational achievement. Yet the kid/man/woman goes through life as just a kid. The mills encourage never-ending childhood, by what they leave out. They, and the rest of our institutions, encourage childish mediocrity as a life. They cannot write, and they do not read. Oh, they can express thoughts with clumsy and primitive writing. They sometimes read a book that's less thought provoking than drinking a beer. Considering the resources that go into "education," the obvious results are pitiful.

Solutions here are even worse than my proposal to outlaw religion. We could probably shake it loose at a big slap by a random selection of removing 50 percent of all college students from their schools. This would be not nearly as bad as sending them off to war, as we do with many of our young men and women. Those who are really talented would likely do well in life anyhow. Among them, those who have a genuine desire for knowledge would find it just as easily as if they were in college. The remaining 50 percent would be required to actually work and learn. For those who find this a problem, they could leave and have their vacancies filled by those who have belatedly learned that they would like to work and learn. It would probably not be very long before the right kids were in college, and the others were out. This is a real opportunity for the market to function, therefore it is undoubtedly unthinkable. This would require some terrible burdens on the college businesses that I will address in another alternative for reform.

At the same time, employers should be made strongly aware that a college degree is by no means necessary for many of the jobs that now require it. This relationship between these two proposals would tend to reinforce each other, as the pool of available degreed people would shrink, and employers would be forced to realistically examine their needs. It would not be a perfect match, so we would need some intelligent, humane way of helping those cut loose from the unnecessary college training. Granted, this reform is a bit rash, but I think it is not really a bad idea.

At the bottom, where it all starts in preschool, we need a new, simple education philosophy. This goes from the bottom to the top, of course. No more, "Get all the education you can, kid," but, "Look, kid, this is your job. You have to work at learning and absorbing. This is not playtime. There are few things in life more satisfying than having a job you love and doing it well. Here is where it starts. If you don't get it here, your chances of getting it at all are very slim."

Perhaps a better alternative to educational reform would be to establish a federal government loan program that would permit any student to go to any college that would admit them, and the loan fund would pay any tuition they needed. The repayment would be levied as a payroll tax collected by IRS and would be set at a rate to reflect the difference in average earnings attributable to a college education versus not having one. The rate could be adjusted upward from a low beginning to a higher level as earning power increases over time. No one could escape repayment without risking prosecution for tax fraud.

To start the program, whatever amount Congress and the president believe is affordable would be appropriated. As there would be more student demand than what would be initially available, a lottery drawing would initiate those selected. After about four years, the fund would begin to be replenished from repayments by graduates. Repayments and appropriations could eventually guarantee a college education for anyone who wants to work for it. Eventually the fund would be self-supporting.

The repayments would carry a modest additional charge to be recalculated annually, somewhat like an adjustable-rate mortgage. The charge would be the allocated expenses of the administering loan agency, with some allowance for losses. Losses would happen from the death of some borrowers. Some may finish college and become Buddhist monks or Catholic nuns. Not much risk of high numbers choosing these paths, but they should be forgiven the debt. They stay in the system, however. Should they later leave the monastery or nunnery for more lucrative employment, they come back into the repayment stream.

Potential borrowers would consider the tuition costs versus the nature of the colleges they are considering, their willingness to carry the debt burden, and their likelihood for success. If they are not doing well or cannot handle the college work, then the pressure to reduce their losses would be beneficial. Those who leave before they earn a degree would pay what they have borrowed under the same arrangements as if they had completed their degrees.

The impact on the colleges would come from two requirements imposed on them. For schools to be on the list for borrower students, they must be able to demonstrate by a standard, uniform accounting format that their athletics expenses are break-even. Tuition cannot include any of the expenses for athletic programs. This would exclude expenses for intramural athletics. It would not include revenues from student fees. This could take good schools out of the competitive attraction of athletics. They could even drop all their formal athletic programs and have only intramural athletics. This would return athletics to its rightful position as a component of real education. The current educational values of sports—dishonesty and violence—would be relieved.

Various arrangements could cover athletics if this is considered important. If tuition were set to cover all instructional costs plus some reasonable uniform overhead, then the athletic resources could be managed by a separate entity. Let the ultimate beneficiaries of these programs, the professional sports organizations, fund them. If indeed alumni love the alma mater for its athletic programs, allow all donations to be directed thereto. As instructional and associated costs are covered by tuition, now the crutch of athletics could be set free. I suspect that a few myths would tumble under these arrangements.

These are not going to be easily calculated arrangements, but the payoffs for society would be great. Experience would refine the accounting for running these institutions. If the colleges and universities cannot figure it all out, then education is in worse shape than I thought.

The second standard is that the school has to have a course grade normal distribution. This would be a great shocker, so a specified time to reach that goal should be allowed.

Third, administrative costs would be limited to some appropriate ratio to instructional costs. This would help to clean out the educational bureaucracy.

We could design a system where education is real, and modest tuition would be paying for it.

We fund public education that is available for all up to the college level. It is not unreasonable to fund college as well, but with appropriate payment placed eventually on the beneficiaries.

It would also place responsibility where it belongs, on the students. That's a shocking thought, but one that in itself would contribute some maturity of attitude rarely found among them. It is also becoming more evident that parents are sacrificing their retirement funds for outrageous tuitions today. This system would surely help deal with that problem too.

An alternative to the tuition program proposal would be simultaneously to establish a really good Internet university for those deeply interested in learning. It would be independent of any bricks, mortar, and ivy school. It would require high standards of performance from faculty and students. Tuition would be charged to cover all costs, but many of the onerous costs of contemporary schools would be foregone. The bureaucracy would be lightly established. There would be no athletic programs. Continual physical plant expansion would not be necessary. Many of the social entertainment programs of colleges would also be absent.

Lectures and notes could be available online and in print. The scourge of textbook expenses for the print notes, or for some just designed for these schools, could be reduced by eliminating multicolor and photographs. Technical progress along these lines would make the learning experience positive. Scattered variations of all the techniques needed are all available now. Each course could include a chat room or rooms for all those who are registered. Should there be sufficient student demand for the proposed university, regular, local, socializing programs could be held.

Making this an excellent educational plant, together with the flexibility and low cost of a genuine educational experience without the associated trash of colleges today, might just inaugurate some real education and, more importantly, real reform. The higher education system is a disgrace today. If we do not change it we are lost.

Making education real is certainly necessary if there are to be any changes that are improvements in the other basics of contemporary life. People will object to my characterizing education as it is, despite so much clear evidence of its failure. One point that has been made to me in discussions is that there are still brilliant students in our colleges. I believe that to be true. I think deterioration has happened at critical positions.

There are still very bright, dedicated students whose proportion in colleges is about the same as ever. Let's say that this is somewhere between 5 percent and 10 percent. It may have declined because of the hostile environment for learning that colleges are today, but maybe not. These people are crucial to a good society. Equally important is the group below them. These are solid students willing to learn. They are not at the summit of intellectual power personally. They are interested, good workers and learners. The first named group and this other group are the combination of educated, motivated men and women who are the core of progress in any society. These are the people who implement and manage the ideas of the higher-level intellectuals. They are the core of all of the important institutions from economics to the arts and everything of value to the genuinely good life. It is here that education has gone wildly astray. Let's say that this proportion of students was something on the order of 25 percent to 30 percent in the past. Today it has virtually disappeared. There are far too few students who take education seriously. It has become a children's game with willing cooperation of the colleges and faculties. The middle group has merged with the always-present bottom group of college students, just there for the hell of it. This does not mean that the intellectual dregs have always been destined for failure. There are other paths to success besides intellectual effort. Losing the middle group destroys the consistent background elements that are the requisites for a decent, well-run society, be it the businesses, museums, churches, or governments. That we still probably have very bright students at about the same ratio of the past is not enough.

Finally, there is one easy way partially to deal with some of these problems. Colleges are now required to report campus crime statistics, though many of them engage in their own petty crimes by inaccurate data. Why not require them to provide their grades distributions as public information? Parents and potential students could compare the distributions with a normal distribution, that is, something on the order of a bell curve. Serious students and parents unwilling to dump thousands of dollars into a playground would move toward the schools with normal grades distributions. Other factors would have to be considered, of course, but this should be a big factor. Accrediting organizations would be required to give these data a place in their evaluations.

Ultimately, there would probably be a correlation of some strength between the normal distribution and the real quality of the school. Further, this could coerce schools into stopping the nonsense of grade escalation, although it's probably at its peak with no further escalation possible. It could be a small step toward making colleges educational institutions again.

15

A Final Note on Our Sorry State

In the end, not only have we created a world where the corporation has ascended to the role of the primary institution, replacing the state as the state replaced the church, but also there are some serious inversions related to this market of a world. I have noted that we no longer distinguish between private and public lives and matters. In broader terms we have inverted and perverted two of the most beautiful and important aspects of humanity, sex and religion. Because every aspect of our lives is for sale, and usually is controlled by corporate interests, there is little that exists at the level of individuals. Privacy is gone and has taken our souls with it. Just think what the world was without television or the Internet. Certainly it was not a saints' paradise, but the reach of the numerous perversities of all kinds, intellectual, spiritual, and physical, was considerably less.

There are many human activities that essentially should be highly personal and private matters. Sex should be a secret loving relationship between two people. Certainly it has been a business since its discovery. We all know of the world's oldest profession, among many other ugly activities related to sex. But we have changed all of these foul endeavors to being accepted generally. Pornography, prostitution, (pardon me, sex workers), and multiple sexual escapades of any variety are viewed benignly as commonplace entertainments and ordinary diversions. Because they are often based in lucrative market returns, their encouragement is as strong as all the wonders of business advertising can sell. Movies, television, and Internet are potent springs from which the reduction of the beauties of sex to tawdry commodities available to everyone is far progressed. There is no shielding. The media reach everywhere. Before these media, a certain amount of containment existed. This is no longer so. We are so sophisticated and open and "sincere." That is to say, we have managed to be the first civilization that has destroyed sex.

We have similarly perverted religion. Again, the same instruments of communication as cited in sex have been at work with religion.

Here is what should be a truly secret loving relationship between a person and God. It cannot even happen without humility, a deep private matter. Again, the media have enhanced the potboiler religions that are nothing but psychology and superstition. No faith is free of this nonsense, but it is not religion.

So sex and religion, the most intensely private matters if they retain their value and beauty, are public circuses. They have had a great push to these descents from their former elevated places by the moneypower continuum.

It seems we need to replace them with large institutions that are private, and we have done that. I noted above that the corporation and its methods and effects have been highly religious. It utilizes the ways of religion and does them better and is more greatly appreciated. But the matter is deeper.

Corporations and governments are supposed to be public institutions. They are required to let us know what they are doing. Yet they have become more secretive and have become private fiefdoms. They are shadow images of what sex and religion should be. So we have found ways to replace the bizarre public conversion of sex and religion from private to public institutions. It is the corporations and our governments whose privileged claims in the continuum are guarded by their illicit secretive ways. Everybody loses because closed government is strongly against democracy, and closed corporations are vehicles for grand theft.

The commonplace scandals of government and corporations receive daily attention in the various media. The reason for their becoming private instead of public is because so many of their activities are illegal, illicit, or disgraceful. Openness would never do.

In addition to these societal perversions, we are, as noted elsewhere, undergoing an institutional evolution paralleling that from when the church was supplanted by the state. One can imagine that this big change from church to state was feared, or at least disliked, by many when it was generally understood. It could be so unsettling on the basis of the magnitude of the change alone. There is more to it than that, and the corporation's supplanting the state is grounds for equal concern. It is also striking that the corrupt church having given in to the state is much like corrupt governments now bowing to the corporation. Even more compelling is that early governments were despotic, so the only initial differences were that the ecclesiastical garments of the despots were traded for the royal garments of the state. The politics of the church were every bit as nasty and harmful to the people as were the politics of the royal state. Eventually more humane government came along in many places.

So it is now with us. The widespread corruption of government is supplanted by the nastiness of corporations. There is not sufficient political awareness that corporate leaders have also taken on the characteristics and attitudes of the terrible royals who followed the nasty church leaders. Corporation leaders live in such ugly and ill-gotten excess that their model predecessors with names followed by roman numerals could not even have imagined at their most decadent. Who knows how long it will take for the corporation to be reigned in to serve humanity? Maybe never.

Any one of our follies and immoralities on its own may not be cause for great concern. It is their cumulative effect, amplified by the widespread adoption of collections of these patterns, that is the problem. As an individual example of the point, if there is a murder on the streets of our cities from time to time, this is a regrettable event. When it is a more than daily occurrence, it is horrible. What becomes more horrible is that we become inured to the problem. It becomes one of those things that happen, just like transportation problems during snowstorms, except that we become angrier about problems created by snowstorms than about the murders.

Addressing a wider view of our lives today, we have been led willingly into levels of irresponsibility and general decadence that are consuming our society. We have become extremely liberal in accepting any form of human behavior, whether it is shown by politicians, corporate executives, university professors, clergy, or the family across the street. We apply no standards to others or to ourselves.

It requires some personal and social discipline to have standards, and the institutions that have usually helped us are all part of the decay. We generally pay scant attention to religion. It is just another commodity for television programming and general marketing. Schools at all levels are nearly worthless and are becoming even worse. We regard freedom as allowing anything to be done that anyone wishes to do, unless there is an economic threat posed by some activity.

The essential difficulty, from which all else follows, is education. It has become such a powerful business at all its levels that, much like any other business that becomes powerful, its minions become arrogant and lose sight of what they are supposed to be doing.

Education is for developing consciousness. The individual, aided by the institutions that have been developed for that purpose, mostly achieves it. It means advancement in intellect, morals, and spirit. We rarely find any serious understanding of those purposes. Many involved could likely not even name them as teachers and administrators. Institutions outside the schools are assuming more educating than are the schools. This is not for the good. Those most influential are shallow despite their influence on us. Television, the Internet, electronic game systems, cell phones, and iPods are the educators. They are educators that usually debase or, at best, trivialize. It is, again, not as though these devices and their systems are a passing phase of childhood. They are embedded in all ages. They are the instruments of our never-ending childhoods.

For most of humanity through most of history, education came from family, nature, and, later, the urban environment. In the sweep of our history, schools are a recent development. Universal education is still not found in most of the world. Where schools are prevalent in a society, even in their earliest days there were always forces working against education. These included lazy students, worldly temptations, bad teachers, poverty, and many other negative influences. So education has always been a struggle against self and external social forces. These were usually mainly individually effective; that is, it was personal.

Today it is different. When we think of developing consciousness in intellectual, spiritual, and moral growth, the forces weighing against this are formidable. Violence and ugliness are the daily themes of television, Internet, and conversation. Very few of us are not exposed regularly to these antitheses of intellectual, spiritual, and moral improvement. Except in the worst of special circumstances, this has not been so for most of our history until now. Even were the formal educational institutional structures dedicated to real purposes, they'd have to fight so hard against these externals. The energy so devoted would leave not enough time for the pursuit of the good. But in one sense, this is not a problem. The system is directed, from teacher to administrator, in the embrace of the ugliness and violence.

Aside from the inherent problems of the named forces, they are character changing in another way. We have become miserly in the pursuit of the interests. Just as the money miser accumulates money well beyond reason, the accumulating of the new forces for our students goes along the same path. It may be that the supermiserly grasp and the gathering of money at the core of our institutions that we accept as something admirable today is related to the miserliness of the experiences of youth.

It is not as though kids get together to play some form of sport as a healthy diversion. It becomes a business discipline. The same is true of time spent on the Internet, on gaming, and on cell phones. The involvement is deep. It is well beyond diversion or entertainment. It is, realistically speaking, life. There is little time or interest available for the genuine articles of education. The noted activities are the actual educators. Family, schools, or any of the other "educators" are shunted aside, both because there is no time for them and for the fascination of the unworthy substitutes. The substitutes sap intellectual and moral energy.

Education in our time is not in crisis. It is in the midst of a catastrophe that continues to grow. Clearly, this rotting of education infects all else in our lives.

As to the corporation as the controlling institution in our lives, we must learn how it should be managed.

Whether yet broadly recognized or not, the corporation as the emerged dominant institution of the world has a place beyond the academic and popular understanding of its role. However troubled and immersed in turmoil, there is little doubt that there is a world society of dimensions never before existing or possible. The reasons don't need another recitation. Historical instruments of management or governing this society are as inappropriate as was the church to handling the societies when it lost out. Multinational quasi-governmental institutions are inadequate for several reasons.

Those in place do not really hold the power they would need, nor is it necessarily desirable that they should. They are fragmented among regional bases and specializations such as the World Bank and the United Nations. Devising something rooted in regular notions of government will not work. That which is to be governed is entirely new. It is also a morass of contentiousness on political, religious, and economic ideas and practices. Some combination of a supranational political (in the traditional sense) institution or a set of them is required. But the central force would be the corporations operating essentially as they now do. The role of the "political" institution would to monitor the operations of the corporations with some authority for control of undesirable tactics and activities. A current example vaguely suggestive of the idea here is the operations of some of the units of the EEU, notably, antitrust enforcement. This not only applies to members but also extends to any corporation wishing to do business in the markets of the EEU countries.

Certainly this is a massive undertaking, not to be designed and implemented quickly. Neither was the EEU. The idea is to create an institution that is capable of dealing with and controlling the undesirable activities of the corporation while allowing and encouraging the enormous powers of the corporation to flourish for the good of the world. Obviously this is a monumental task. But the emergence of the state over the church, in hindsight, was an equally difficult task.

The idea here is to use the most flexible, changeable, capable device—the corporation—to advance humanity in the superglobal environment in which we are now immersed. If we do not, it may take over without properly being defined in its place with humanity. This would be disastrous. Our attitude in this endeavor should be roughly like the well-known story about Lyndon Johnson. When someone called a political ally of his a bastard, he replied, "Yes, he was, but he is our bastard." This sets the frame for the future of the corporation in the role I envision. Many of them are bastards. We have to make them our bastards, and more ours, than bastards.

References

Berle and Means, *The Modern Corporation and Private Property*

Blum and Kalven, *The Uneasy Case for Progressive Taxation*

Bogle, J. *The Battle for the Soul of Capitalism*

Bury, J. B. *The Idea of Progress*

Heller, J. *Catch-22*

Hildegard of Bingen. *Scivias*

Johnson, H. *The Best of Times*

Journal of Quantitative Finance (December 2004)

Kessner,
Capital City: New York City and the Men Behind America's Rise to Economic Dominance 1860-1900
Leach, *Land of Desire*

Merton, *The Seeds of Contemplation*

Mc Fadden, J. *Quantum Evolution*

Phillips, K. *American Theocracy*

Rubenstein, *Aristotle's Children*

Satherthwaite, A. *Going Shopping*

Walras, L. *Elements of Pure Economics*

Zollo, R. *I Wrote to Mussolini*

www.ingramcontent.com/pod-product-compliance
Lightning Source LLC
Chambersburg PA
CBHW031054180526
45163CB00002BA/826